Practical English for International Shipping and Port Business

国际港航实用业务英语

李爱云　王学锋　主　编
　　　　　贾行浩　副主编

人民交通出版社股份有限公司
China Communications Press Co.,Ltd.

内 容 提 要

本教材用通俗易懂、简单实用的语言介绍国际港航运输业务操作规范,强调英语学习听说读写练交替循环,有机融合,重在培养学生运用英语处理国际港航运输业务的能力,突出岗位能力需求与教学内容和教学模式相对接。

图书在版编目(CIP)数据

国际港航实用业务英语 / 李爱云,王学锋主编.—北京:人民交通出版社股份有限公司,2018.12(2025.1重印)
 ISBN 978-7-114-14678-7

Ⅰ.①国… Ⅱ.①李… ②王… Ⅲ.①国际航运—英语 Ⅳ.①F551

中国版本图书馆 CIP 数据核字(2018)第 089836 号

Guoji Ganghang Shiyong Yewu Yingyu

书　　名:	国际港航实用业务英语
著 作 者:	李爱云　王学锋
责任编辑:	刘永芬　朱明周
责任校对:	张　贺
责任印制:	张　凯
出版发行:	人民交通出版社股份有限公司
地　　址:	(100011)北京市朝阳区安定门外外馆斜街 3 号
网　　址:	http://www.ccpcl.com.cn
销售电话:	(010)85285911
总 经 销:	人民交通出版社股份有限公司发行部
经　　销:	各地新华书店
印　　刷:	北京科印技术咨询服务有限公司数码印刷分部
开　　本:	787×1092　1/16
印　　张:	13.75
字　　数:	320 千
版　　次:	2018 年 12 月　第 1 版
印　　次:	2025 年 1 月　第 2 次印刷
书　　号:	ISBN 978-7-114-14678-7
定　　价:	42.00 元

(有印刷、装订质量问题的图书由本公司负责调换)

前　言

　　国际港航业务英语是专业特色十分显著的行业英语，具有国际港航业务与英语交叉融合的特点。本书依据国际集装箱班轮公司开展集装箱海运出口"Door to Door"全程运输服务流程，设置12个单元模块：集装箱航运概况、揽货、接受订舱、发放空箱、装箱、接收重箱、通关、港口货物作业、港口理货、提单签发、货物到港及交付、货损及索赔。每单元内容紧紧围绕所对应岗位工作职责，从业务须知(Basic Knowledge Concerned)、业务信函(Business Letters)、业务情景对话(Situational Dialogue)、业务单证(Related Documents)四个角度立体式地展现了用英语沟通业务、处理工作任务的真实工作场景。

　　本教材采用通俗易懂、简单实用的语言介绍国际港航运输业务操作规范，强调英语学习听说读写练交替循环、有机融合，重在培养学生运用英语处理国际港航运输业务的能力，突出岗位能力需求与教学内容和教学模式相对接。

编　者
2017 年 9 月

目　录

Unit 1　Overview of Container Shipping(集装箱航运概况) ················· 1
　　Part A：Basic Knowledge Concerned ································· 3
　　Part B：Business Letters ·· 7
　　Part C：Situational Dialogue ·· 11
　　Exercises ··· 15

Unit 2　Cargo Canvassing(揽货) ·· 19
　　Part A：Basic Knowledge Concerned ································ 21
　　Part B：Business Letters ··· 25
　　Part C：Situational Dialogue ······································· 28
　　Part D：Related Documents ·· 30
　　Exercises ·· 33

Unit 3　Booking Acceptance(接受订舱) ·································· 37
　　Part A：Basic Knowledge Concerned ································ 39
　　Part B：Business Letters ··· 44
　　Part C：Situational Dialogue ······································· 47
　　Part D：Related Documents ·· 49
　　Exercises ·· 52

Unit 4　Empty Container Release(发放空箱) ······························ 55
　　Part A：Basic Knowledge Concerned ································ 57
　　Part B：Business Letters ··· 63
　　Part C：Situational Dialogue ······································· 64
　　Part D：Shipping Documents ······································· 66
　　Exercises ·· 67

Unit 5　Containers Stuffing(装箱) ······································ 71
　　Part A：Basic Knowledge Concerned ································ 73
　　Part B：Business Letters ··· 76

Part C: Situational Dialogue	78
Part D: Shipping Documents	80
Exercises	82

Unit 6　Laden Containers Gate-in(接收重箱)　85

Part A: Basic Knowledge Concerned	87
Part B: Business Letters	91
Part C: Situational Dialogue	93
Part D: Shipping Documents	94
Exercises	96

Unit 7　Customs Clearance(通关)　101

Part A: Basic Knowledge Concerned	103
Part B: Business Letters	105
Part C: Situational Dialogue	108
Part D: Relevant Documents	110
Exercises	112

Unit 8　Cargo Handling at Container Port(港口货物作业)　117

Part A: Basic Knowledge Concerned	119
Part B: Business Letters	125
Part C: Situational Dialogue	128
Part D: Related Documents	130
Exercises	132

Unit 9　Tally Work(港口理货作业)　135

Part A: Basic Knowledge Concerned	137
Part B: Business Letters	140
Part C: Situational Dialogue	141
Part D: Related Documents	144
Exercises	145

Unit 10　B/L Issuance(签发提单)　149

Part A: Basic Knowledge Concerned	151
Part B: Business Letters	154
Part C: Situational Dialogue	156
Part D: Related Documents	159

  Exercises ·· 160

Unit 11 Cargo Arrival and Delivery(货物到港及交付) ··························· 163

  Part A：Basic Knowledge Concerned ·· 165

  Part B：Business Letters ·· 171

  Part C：Situational Dialogue ·· 175

  Part D：Shipping Documents ·· 179

  Exercises ·· 181

Unit 12 Cargo Damage and Claim(货损及索赔) ·· 185

  Part A：Basic Knowledge Concerned ·· 187

  Part B：Business Letters ·· 192

  Part C：Situational Dialogue ·· 194

  Part D：Related Documents ·· 197

  Exercises ·· 198

Keys to the Exercises ·· 201

References ··· 210

Unit 1　Overview of Container Shipping
（集装箱航运概况）

Overview of Container Shipping
（集装箱航运概况） Unit 1

Part A: Basic Knowledge Concerned

Text 1: Containerization

Containerization* is a system of standardized transport, which uses a common size of steel container to transport goods. These containers can easily be transferred between different modes of transport — container ships to lorries and trains. This makes transport and trade of goods cheaper and more efficient.

The container was invented in 1956 by Malcom Maclean, an American truck businessman. International standards for container sizes were established between 1968 and 1970. The widespread adoption* of containers enabled an improvement in trade and contributed to the process of globalization. About 90% of non-bulk goods are carried in containers. 27% of containers originate from China, the world's largest exporter of manufactured goods.

The humble container may look a very simple factor of production, but it is credited with radically improving the efficiency of trade, enabling a significant boost* in efficiency and economic growth. Before the use of containers, goods would be exported in a mixture of bags and boxes. It meant that loading and unloading took longer and was hard work. A large workforce was required to unload and sort the goods on arrival, before repacking for the onward transport.

The widespread use of containers helped to significantly reduce the cost of trade.

- Unloading goods could be streamlined* — less labour was needed, significantly boosting labour productivity. In 1965 dock labour could move only 1.7 tons per hour onto a cargo ship; five years later (1970), they could load 30 tons in an hour.

- The increased labour productivity reduced the power of organized labour on the ship front, which could often paralyze trade (It's fiction but *On the Waterfront* is a great film about organized labour on the docks, with some elements of truth).

containerization
n. 集装箱化

扫码看视频
"集装箱改变世界"

adoption
n. 采用

boost
v. 推动，促进，增加

streamline
v. 使流线型，使精简

secure *adj.* 安全的	• Containerization is much more secure*. When goods were transported loose, it was much easier for goods to go missing. There is an old joke that the wages of a docking worker were £50 a week, plus all the whiskey you could carry home. Containers made transporting goods safer and more secure. Lower incidence of theft also reduced the cost of insurance.
downside *n.* 缺点 contraband *n.* 走私货，禁运品	However, as a downside*, it is said containers have made it easier to smuggle contraband* and illegal goods. • The container principle. If you increase the surface area of a shape, the volume increases at a more than proportional rate. If you double the surface area, the volume of goods that can be transported could increase the volume four fold. The new containers enabled an exploitation of this principle because they were larger than previous small boxes.
standardization *n.* 标准化	• Increased standardization*. The size of containers were standardized at a series of conferences in the late 1960s. There are many benefits of international standardization. It helps in standardizing transport, such as lorries, fork lift trucks* and all the paraphernalia* of transport.
fork lift truck *n.* 叉车 paraphernalia *n.* 用具，装备	• Because containers were quicker to load, it encouraged the building of bigger "container ships". Larger loads could be offloaded in a shorter time. This reduced the cost of ship transport and enabled transport economies of scale.
innovation *n.* 创新，革新	The container may appear very "low tech", but it shows that even low tech innovations* can have large benefit when implemented internationally. The real strength of the container is helping to reduce costs, improve trade and increase the efficiency of international trade. Of course, there have been many other factors boosting international trade, such as lower tariffs, the growth of emerging economies, but the container has played an important role in this aspect of trade.
	Text 2: How Liner Shipping Works
liner *n.* 班轮	Liner* shipping is the service of transporting goods by means of high-capacity, ocean-going ships that transit regular routes on fixed

schedules. There are approximately 400 liner services, most sailing weekly, in operation today. Liner vessels, primarily in the form of containerships and roll-on/roll-off* ships, carry about 60 percent of the goods by value moved internationally by sea each year.

roll-on/roll-off
滚装式

Container Shipping in Ten Steps

Every day, thousands of containers arrive at seaports from countries all around the world. They are carried aboard liner ships, which offer regularly scheduled service on fixed routes—much like a bus or train service does. Each shipment represents a specific supply chain, whether it is patio furniture from Thailand bound for a Milan retailer or as illustrated here—shoes shipped from China to an athletic supply store in Europe or North America. Every supply chain is somewhat unique* because it involves the timely and accurate transfer of goods between various modes of transport. Goods transported by ocean containers on liner ships can be placed into the container at the factory origin. The container is locked and sealed so the goods can remain safely secured inside the container until it arrives at the purchaser's warehouse, factory or store. For this reason, more than 50 percent of the value of goods moved internationally by sea is now moving in containers on liner ships.

unique
adj. 独特的

① An athletic supply store is running low on the season's hot, new shoes, which are manufactured in northern China. The store places an order for 500 pairs. The shoe company works with a freight forwarder to arrange transport from the Chinese factory for the shipment of shoes.

② A trucking company arrives at the Chinese factory, loads the order, along with orders from many other retailers, into a 40-foot container, which is bolted shut and fitted with a high-security seal. The container will not be opened again until it arrives at a distribution warehouse in the destination country, unless customs officials decide to open and inspect it.

③ The freight forwarder deter mines it is most economical to truck the container to the Port of Tianjin. The freight forwarder has contracted with a container shipping line, which must submit documentation about the shipment to government authorities in the exporting and importing countries. This "manifest data" includes information such as exact contents, the exporter, the importer and who is transporting the cargo.

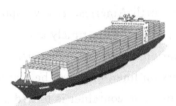

④ Now loaded onto a container ship, the container of shoes is bound for a discharge port on another continent far away.

⑤ A few days before the ship is scheduled to arrive at the destination port, the captain of the vessel provides a report to the government of the destination country that contains information about the ship, its crew and its cargo.

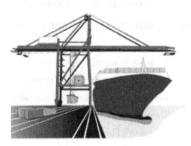

⑥ Having received proper clearance to arrive at the port, the container vessel docks at a berth adjacent to large cranes that will be used to unload the containers of cargo.

⑦ Many dock workers—sometimes more than 100 per vessel arrive to work the ship. They include crane operators, lashers, clerks and cargo equipment operators.

⑧ Customs officials, armed with a careful evaluation of each container's documentation, may select specific containers for further inspection.

Overview of Container Shipping
（集装箱航运概况） Unit 1

⑨ Once cleared by customs, workers load the container onto a special truck trailer or chassis. Now the container of shoes can be trucked to the distribution center. Containers are often transported by train when the destination is a long distance from the port.

⑩ The truck arrives at an import distributing center located not too far from the port, where the container is opened and the orders by individual stores are separated and prepared for shipment. The next day, the athletic supply store receives its 500 pairs of the season's most popular athletic shoes.

Part B: Business Letters

Sample 1: Letter from the CEO

Dear reader,

I am pleased to present you with our Sustainability Progress Update 2012.

Container shipping is a facilitator of global trade and an integral part of the global economy. Much like the global economy, the container shipping industry has been subject to significant volatility* over the past 5-10 years.

volatility
n. 波动

In BCD Line, we have gone from record losses in one year (2009) to record profits in the next (2010) and the last two years have also been highly volatile. Changing this is a priority for BCD Line; stable satisfactory financial results are a must for any business. Given our role in global trade, we also believe that societies and markets would be better served by a container shipping industry that is less volatile and more financially sustainable*.

sustainable
adj. 可持续的

In 2012 we have taken important steps to bring BCD Line on a path to sustainable profitable growth. For example, we have managed our capacity* to better match the demand in the market and we have reduced our costs through an ongoing focus on energy efficiency.

Our CO_2 performance has never been better, but we still see significant potential for further improvements as our new and more efficient Triple-E ships enter into service in 2013 and 2014. Based on our performance over the past 5 years, we feel confident setting a new target for 2020 — a 40% reduction of CO_2 emissions* per container · kilometer, using 2007 as our baseline.

During the past year, we have also worked hard to make BCD Line a safer place to work. Unfortunately, we still face challenges. In 2012, we had four fatalities* — two that were work-related and two that resulted from a criminal act. Any fatality is — and remains — unacceptable. It is our clear target to bring the number of fatalities down to zero. We are also working hard to minimize the number of work-related accidents.

In 2012, we saw an increasing number of customers engage with us on sustainability. We welcome and encourage this interest and hope to see much more of it in 2013. An increased demand for shipping services with a strong sustainability profile will help drive industry-wide change, thereby enabling more sustainable global trade.

Best wishes,

Jimmy King

CEO, BCD Liner Business

Sample 2: Customer Advisory — Liner Shipping Alliance Developments

Dear Customers,

NYK Line acknowledges the announcement by CMA CGM, China Cosco Shipping, Evergreen Line and OOCL that they will form a new liner shipping alliance* upon the cessation of the existing O3 and CHKYE alliance agreements at the end of March 2017.

---

capacity
n. 运力

emission
n. 排放

fatality
n. 致命性

liner shipping alliance
班轮联盟

We wish to reassure our customers that this is an expected development in the context of the alliance realignment activity which results from the recent mergers and acquisitions* in our industry.

acquisition
n. 收购

This development in no way disadvantages NYK Line nor hampers* our ability to deliver a full range of competitive products to our customers in either the short or long term.

hamper
v. 妨碍

The G6 Alliance and its existing product portfolio* will continue to operate until the official dissolution of the alliance in April 2017.

portfolio
n. 组合

Negotiations relating to our future alliance position are on-going. NYK Line views the opportunity to review and adjust our alliance agreements as a constructive development and we are absolutely confident of a positive outcome. Transition, when it occurs, will be well planned, smooth and of minimal impact to our customers.

The NYK Group remains committed to its long standing involvement in liner shipping. The strength of this unwavering commitment is evidenced by our investment in new state of the art ULCS (14,000 TEU) vessels which will be added to our fleet over the course of the next few years, extensive investments in the new technology, container equipment and cost optimization initiatives across our liner business.

Further information on a future alliance and products will be made available to our customers as soon as it becomes available. We fully appreciate the interest in these developments and the need for product detail awareness in order to facilitate longer term supply chain planning.

NYK Line looks forward to continuing to drive innovation in our industry and to provide a broad portfolio of liner services far into the future.

We wish to thank all our loyal, highly valued customers for their continued support!

Yours faithfully,
NYK Global Liner Management Division

Sample 3: Merger of Hapag-Lloyd and UASC

Dear Hapag-Lloyd and UASC Customers,

Today, we are proud to announce that Hapag-Lloyd and United Arab Shipping Company have completed the merger to become a combined company. This is a major milestone* in the history of the both companies as we continue to evolve to meet customer's needs and adapt to market conditions.

In the "new" Hapag-Lloyd, one of the top 5 global carriers, we will be ready to deliver a number of important added benefits to you, including an extensive global network — now with added focus in the Middle East — making us capable of serving you even better, globally and locally. The combined company also boasts a larger, more efficient, and environmentally friendly fleet of vessels, allowing us to deploy* the most effective vessel class in each of the trade lanes. Well-trained and experienced teams will be available to handle your cargo in an office near you, now with even deeper insights into your business. A financially solid business partner backed by a strong group of diversified shareholders will ensure your cargo is in safe hands at all times.

For the immediate future, the two companies will continue to operate independently as we work to integrate our internal systems and processes as quickly as possible. We therefore kindly ask you to continue working with your current Hapag-Lloyd/UASC counterparts in Sales, Customer Service, Operations and Finance. We will transfer the first UASC services to Hapag-Lloyd from mid-July followed by the remaining services gradually over several weeks. Bookings for these services in Hapag-Lloyd's systems will commence well in advance.

Over the course of the next few days, your Hapag-Lloyd or UASC account representative will contact you to explain what this will mean for your business and what you can expect in the coming weeks. Ensuring a smooth transition for you is our top priority. With two large, successful mergers in recent years, we have an industry-leading track record for conducting integrations* rapidly and efficiently — and are confident of achieving this goal again.

---

milestone
n. 里程碑

deploy
v. 部署,配置

integration
n. 集成,整合

Overview of Container Shipping
（集装箱航运概况） Unit 1

Your feedback is important to help us safeguard a continued successful relationship now and in the future.

We will provide regular updates about the progress of the integration of both companies through a weekly transition newsletter, which will also be published on *www.hapag-lloyd.com* and *www.uasc.net*. Should you have any immediate enquiries, please feel free to send us an e-mail at *better.united@hlag.com*.

We would like to thank you for your continued support and loyalty during the integration period and we look forward to serving you even better!

Rolf Habben Jansen, CEO Hapag-Lloyd

Jørn Hinge, President & CEO UASC

Thorsten Haeser, CCO Hapag-Lloyd

Uffe Ostergaad, CCO UASC

Part C: Situational Dialogue

Scene 1: Talking About Mode of Transport

A: Good morning, Bill. I really have some trouble about how to transport my goods to foreign country since this is my first time to do a foreign trade transaction. Would you tell me how to make business more profitable?

B: Don't be nervous. You can first take account for the modes of transport, and then try to find a good transport company or a freight forwarder.

A: Certainly, We are thinking about this. But which transportation means is the most favorable?

B: Generally speaking, ocean freight is the most widely used form of transportation in international trade. In China and most other foreign countries, it is generally considered as a cheap mode of transport for delivering large quantities of goods over long

扫码听音频

— 11 —

distances.

A: Oh! That's why most companies like to choose a marine liner to deliver their goods.

B: That's it. Since the procedures for shipment of goods are rather complex, most companies do not attend to all the details of shipment themselves. They are inclined to use the services of shipping and forwarding agents.

A: But what do they depend on?

B: The method used depends on time and cost.

A: Could you help me to analyze it in details when shipping happens?

B: Trains are usually used to transport bulk products that are low in value and must travel great distances. Trucks can stop within a city and deliver goods directly to the market.

A: And then that is to say, air freight is quicker?

B: Yes, but it is more expensive. When speed is taken into consideration, this will be more effective. Food and some urgently needed goods are usually delivered by it.

A: What about ships?

B: That is just what I want to tell you. Since you export chemical goods, you'd do better to try this means. Commodities such as coal, grain, chemicals and iron ore are often shipped by this means. Although it is a little slower, it is much cheaper. So far, most of our export goods have been transported by ship.

A: Thank you. You have enlightened me.

B: That's all right.

Scene 2: Talking About Liner Service and Tramp Service

A: There are two types of ocean shipping services—liners and tramps*.

B: Could you please introduce them respectively?

A: A liner sails on schedule dates between a fixed group of ports.

扫码听音频

liner and tramp
定期和不定期

B: What about tramps?

A: A tramp usually trades in various ports in search of cargo.

B: Who will take the responsibilities to book shipping space*?

book shipping space
订舱

A: It often depends on the trade terms agreed between the seller and buyer. Under CIF terms, the seller may contact directly with the shipping company for a liner or a tramp. Or to save time and trouble, he may employ the services of a forwarding agent.

B: What is the duty of the forwarding agent?

A: The forwarding agent should collect the consignment, arrange shipment, handle all documentation, send shipping advice and so on.

B: Is there any contract between the forwarding agent and the exporter?

A: Of course. The contract indicates that the goods are loaded on board a ship or placed under the control of the shipping company.

Scene 3: Talking About Container and Shipping

A: Can you tell me something about the container and shipping?

B: Of course. With the expansion of international trade, the container service has become popular. The use of containers provides a highly efficient form of transport by road, rail and air though its fullest benefits are felt in shipping, where costs may be reduced by as much as one half.

扫码听音频

A: What is the container made of?

B: Containers are constructed of metal and are of standard lengths ranging from ten to forty feet.

A: Is there any benefit?

B: Of course. The container can be loaded and locked at factory premises or at nearby container bases, making pilferage* impossible. There is no risk of goods getting lost or mislaid in transit.

pilferage
n. 偷盗

A: Oh, I know. Manpower in handling is greatly reduced, with lower costs and less risk of damage. Temperature-controlled containers are provided for the types of cargo that need them.

B: You are right. Mechanical handling enables cargo to be loaded in a matter of hours rather than days, thus reducing the time ships spent in port and greatly increasing the number of sailings.

Supplement: The Development of Liner Shipping Alliance

Graph 1: Current Alliance (as of 18 July 2016)

2M — Maersk Line and Mediterranean Shipping Co. announced the 10-year 2M Alliance vessel-sharing agreement on the Asia-Europe, trans-Pacific and trans-Atlantic trades as the carriers strived to better utilize capacity in the wake of their failed bid to launch the P3 Network in 2014.

O3 — The "Ocean Three" Alliance among CMA CGM, China Shipping and United Arab Shipping Co.

G6 Alliance — The G6 Alliance members are APL, Hapag-Lloyd, Hyundai Merchant Marine, MOL, NYK Line and Orient Overseas Container Line. Like the 2M Alliance and CKYHE Alliance, the G6 Alliance is a vessel-sharing agreement that allows container lines to achieve economies of scale and better cope with periods of slack demand. The G6 Alliance will cease operation in 2017 as its members enter new agreements.

Overview of Container Shipping
（集装箱航运概况） Unit 1

CKYHE Alliance—The CKYHE Alliance consists of Cosco Container Lines, "K" Line, Yang Ming Line, Hanjin Shipping, and Evergreen Line. The CKYHE Alliance will cease to operate in 2017 as a result of consolidation in the container shipping industry. Evergreen Line will join the Ocean Alliance along with Cosco, which merged with China Shipping Container Lines in 2015, while "K" Line, Yang Ming Line, and Hanjin are joining THE Alliance.

Graph 2: Upcoming Alliance Reorganization (as of Jan 2017 and onward)

THE Alliance—THE Alliance consists of NYK Line, MOL, "K" Line, Hapag-Lloyd, and Yang Ming Line. The capacity of United Arab Shipping Company is also included in THE Alliance because of its expected merger with Hapag-Lloyd.

Ocean Alliance—The Ocean Alliance brings together the recently formed China Cosco Shipping, with Evergreen Line, CMA CGM, and OOCL in a vessel- and slot-sharing agreement. The formation of this alliance means that the members of the other major alliances, the G6, CKYHE, and Ocean Three, will need to form new VSAs with different carriers, creating another level of uncertainty in the shipping industry.

Exercises

Task 1: Listen to the following text and fill in each blank with one or two appropriate words.

Containerization is preferred over the conventional modes of transportation which fundamentally takes the place of liner bulk cargo transportation in recent several decades.

The main ____①____ of containerization are listed as follows:

- Containerization can considerably raise the cargo-handling productively. The ____②____ of the mechanical and automatic means accelerates the loading and unloading of containers. The ____③____ of container-handling has reached 50 TEU per hour.

- Containerization can reduce the cargo discrepancy and ____④____. Thanks to the protection of containers with high-strength and water-proof and door-to-door transportation, the missing and damage of cargo during moving is evidently ____⑤____.

- Containerization has realized quick ____⑥____ between ships and other transportation. Therefore, it is a very highly ____⑦____ method not only for marine transportation but also for inland transportation.

- Containerization can largely reduce the overall cost and expense of transportation. The reduction is not only shown in ____⑧____ (packing cost, storage cost, tally fees, etc.) but also in cargo-handling costs.

There are various kinds of ____⑨____ employed in the handling of containers, such as container gantry crane, container trucks and chassis(semi-trailer), straddle carrier, container forklift, rubber-tired gantry crane(RTG), rail-mounted gantry crane (RMG), front-handling stacker, etc.

The container gantry crane (portainer) is used to discharge containers from ships, and then the containers are ____⑩____ to the storage yard by semi-trailers. Straddle carriers are used to transfer containers between marshalling yards and ships. Containers are ____⑪____ by forklifts or front-handling stackers, and can be transferred between different transportation by RMG or RTG on the yard.

Containers can be divided into several types according to their ____⑫____. They are dry cargo container, bulk container, reefer container, open-top container, plat-form based container, tank container and car container, etc.

Task 2: Fill in each blank with the most appropriate word given below in its right form.

capacity	equivalent	regular	variety	charter
weekly	overcapacity	integration	competitive	share

1. Liner shipping is the service of transporting goods by means of high-capacity, ocean-going ships that transit _____ routes on fixed schedules.

Overview of Container Shipping
（集装箱航运概况） Unit 1

2. According to Alphaliner, the global container fleet had a total _____ of almost 17 million TEU in July 2013.

3. The alliance will bring service reliability and _____ of the latest vessels in a fleet of more than 350 container ships.

4. Formed by Denmark's Maersk Line and Switzerland's Mediterranean Shipping Co SA, 2M started its operations in 2015, and controls more than 2.1 million twenty-foot _____ units, and manages more than 200 vessels.

5. Ocean Alliance will enable each member to offer _____ products and comprehensive service networks covering the Asia-Europe, Asia-Mediterranean, Asia-Red Sea, Asia-Middle East, trans-Pacific, Asia-North America East Coast, and trans-Atlantic routes.

6. Alliance members will also _____ coordinated sailing schedules, commercial information and land-based logistics networks which can help cut costs.

7. In addition, slow economic growth in both developed and developing markets has caused more than one-third of _____ of vessels.

8. Because most containership services operate on a _____ basis and call at the same ports every week, each service uses several container ships (generally anywhere from four to twelve) of a similar size.

9. Container ship operators can either deploy ships that they own, or they can _____ the ships for operation from a ship broker.

10. Container ships come in a _____ of sizes and have grown increasingly larger over time.

Task 3: Translate the following terms.

1. shipping alliance
2. containerization
3. ship operator
4. CO_2 emissions
5. vessel-sharing agreement
6. 运输方式
7. 班轮运输
8. 海运承运人
9. 供应链
10. 集装箱船

Task 4: Supply the missing words in the blanks of the following letter. The first letters are given.

APL stops Booking and Loading on Hanjin Vessels

Dear Valued Customer,

As you might have read in the news, Hanjin has filed for court receivership.

With immediate e ____①____ (生效), APL has stopped loading on Hanjin ships.

APL is currently working with the G6 a ____②____ （联盟）while Hanjin operates in another alliance for the major East-West trades. Our services remain u ____③____（不受影响）, except for the Asia South America (ASA) and West Med Service (WMS), for which Hanjin has one ship d ____④____（配置）in each.

APL is working closely with our remaining partners to secure replacement ships in order to maintain the weekly, r ____⑤____（可靠的）and consistent service offerings in the aforementioned ASA and WMS services.

Hanjin's difficulties underline the tough operating environment that the l____⑥____（班轮）industry has been facing for a while now. In spite of this, APL, now a part of the CMA CGM Group, will continue, as always, to fulfil our c____⑦____（承诺）to you in these challenging times. We thank you for your continued business and s____⑧____（支持）.

Sincerely,

APL

Unit 2　Cargo Canvassing
（揽货）

Part A: Basic Knowledge Concerned

Text 1: What is Freight Prepaid or Freight Collect

The term freight* used here refers to transportation charges. The INCOTERMS 2010 (International Commercial Terms) determine whether the shipper or the consignee is responsible for paying the freight.

Freight Prepaid

Freight prepaid means the freight has been paid or prepaid by the shipper. The trade terms—CFR, CIF, CPT, CIP, DDP, DAT and DAP—require a prepayment of the cost of main carriage.

In a prepaid delivery, the letter of credit (L/C) normally requires that the words "Freight Prepaid*" be marked on the Bill of Lading (B/L), clearly indicating payment or prepayment of freight at port (or point) of origin. The mark may appear by stamp or be indicated by other means. The words "freight to be prepaid" or "freight prepayable" or similar wording that may appear on the B/L do not prove that the freight has been paid.

In a prepaid delivery by a courier, the transport document (i.e., the courier's receipt) issued by a courier or expedited delivery service must show that the courier charges have been paid or prepaid by the shipper.

Freight Collect*

Freight collect means that the freight still has to be paid by the consignee. The trade terms—FOB, FAS, EXW and FCA—require a collection of the cost of the main carriage.

In a collect delivery, the letter of credit (L/C) normally requires that the words "Freight Collect" be marked on the Bill of Lading, clearly indicating freight payable at destination. The mark may appear by stamp* or be indicated by other means.

A collection charge usually is included in the freight rate or is collected separately. Hence, the freight charged on a collect basis is normally higher than on a prepaid basis.

---

freight
n. 运费

freight prepaid
运费预付

freight collect
运费到付

stamp
n. 印章

Text 2: What You Should Know When Requesting an Ocean Freight Quote

Ocean freight is one of the biggest costs for importers today, and it's not exactly getting any cheaper. Ocean freight cost has been and is steadily increasing, which makes it hold a bigger and bigger piece of importers' overall expenses. For this reason, it is critical to know how to calculate the shipping cost. It is so important to provide the most complete information to your transportation partner when requesting a quote*, in order to get the most accurate ocean freight cost.

Origin/Destination

The most basic required information is to know where the cargo needs to be picked up and where it needs to be delivered. Pay attention to your agreement with your supplier, and find out what exactly your supplier is responsible for. Are they only loading the container, and it needs to be picked up* from the factory/warehouse or are they delivering the container to the closest port?

Equipment/Container Size

The most commonly used containers are 20 ft., 40 ft. and 40 ft. high cube. Your supplier can provide this information according to the amount of goods you have ordered, or you can check with your forwarder.

Transit Time*

Inform your forwarder if you need a fast service or not. Some carriers have longer transit time with better rates, and significant cost savings can be made if your shipment is not time sensitive.

Merchandise Ready Date

This is also very important information to have. Ocean freight rates are seasonal and change frequently. Even if you don't have an exact date, provide an estimate.

Customs Clearance*

Customs clearance needs to be done at the destination country according to country regulations. Ask your forwarder if they

---

quote
n. 报价

pick up
提取

transit time
运输时间

customs clearance
清关

provide that service. If not, find a broker and request a separate rate from them.

Charges at Destination

As each country has their own regulations, just as each port has different charges. Find out if there are any additional charges at the port of destination.

Door Delivery*

If you need to deliver the container to a specific address, provide the full address to your forwarder to get an exact door delivery rate. Try to determine how long it would take to unload the container at the final destination. This can prove to be an extra cost, as most truckers give 2 hours free time then charge by the hour after that.

door delivery
送货上门

Commodity

Always inform your forwarder about the product that you are shipping. If it's a hazardous* shipment, it requires special permits to carry the cargo.

hazardous
adj. 危险的

In order to know the market, you have to do your research. Contact several freight forwarders for rates, to get a good idea of the current rate level and whether or not your current transportation partner is providing you with competitive* rates. This doesn't mean that you base your decision on who provides the lowest rates. Many other factors are important when choosing service providers.

competitive
adj. 有竞争力的

You can ask for references if you are considering working with a new forwarder. A freight forwarder that has slightly higher rates, but excellent references can serve you better than one that provides low rates but takes 3 days to respond to your emails or return your call.

Text 3: Freight Shipping Rates and Container Costs

The total price for a shipment consists of various components: a basic rate, mandatory* surcharges and extra services.

Below you'll find a short description of each of the main

mandatory
adj. 强制的，义务的

components, enabling you—if needed—to better understand the price structure and even the breakdown on your invoice.

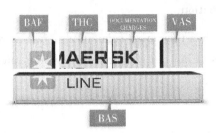

The Basic Ocean Freight

basic ocean freight
基本海运费

The Basic Ocean Freight* (OCF) is a transportation rate for moving your cargo. The rate is determined by varying factors such as the different origin-destination combinations and the cargo type (Dry Cargo or Reefer Cargo).

The Mandatory Surcharges

A mandatory "surcharge" constitutes a part of the rate which is not covered by the basic ocean freight. Mandatory surcharges are established to cover cost items or services that are either pass-through charges (e. g. from terminals) or beyond the basic ocean transport services. These surcharges are applicable to every shipment.

Below you'll find more information about the most frequent surcharges.

- **Bunker Adjustment Factor.**

BAF
燃油附费，燃油调整因素

The Bunker Adjustment Factor (BAF)* is a charge to account for the fluctuations in bunker costs (oil used by the vessels) that changes on quarterly basis.

- **Terminal Handling Charges.**

THC
码头操作费

Terminal Handling Charges (THC)* are based on the cost of handling the container in the terminals, including loading and discharging containers to/from the vessel.

- **Low Sulphur Surcharge.**

LSS
低硫附加费

The Low Sulphur Surcharge (LSS)* covers the expenses related to the usage of low-sulphur fuel with a maximum sulphur content of 0.1% used in shipments transported completely or partially across the Sulphur Emission Control Areas.

- **Peak Season Surcharge.**
  The Peak Season Surcharge (PSS)* is a seasonal fee applied during high volume shipping periods in certain trades. The fee is applicable to all shipments that move in these trades during the high volume periods.

  PSS
  旺季附加费

- **Emergency Risk Surcharge.**
  The Emergency Risk Surcharge (ERS)* covers additional costs faced by the carrier when moving cargo in dangerous regions including those that are threatened by hazards, violence or piracy*. The fee will be applied to bookings that are from, to or transited through the affected areas.

  ERS
  应急风险附加费

  piracy
  海盗

- **Documentation Charges.**
  Documentation Charges are a service whereby carriers provide shippers with the necessary transport documents for you at the origin and destination, based on shipping instructions.

Value Added Services

Value Added Services (VAS) are extra services that we offer to accommodate your additional requirements.

Examples of Value Added Services are: Container Cleaning, Garments on Hangers*, Out of Gauge*, Controlled Atmosphere, Cold Treatment, Genset*.

garments on hangers
挂衣柜

out of gauge
超标，超限

genset
发电机

Part B: Business Letters

Sample 1: FCL Freight Rates Inquiry

Dear Sir,

It would be very kind of you if you please let us know the present freight rate for cased leather shoes for shipment from Mumbai to London.

With this kindly also inform us of the frequency of your sailings and the approximate time of your voyage.

Yours Faithfully,

×××（Company name）

Sample 2: Reply to the Letter of Inquiry Regarding Freight Rates

Dear Sir,

With reference to your letter of 15th instant, we are pleased to inform you that our present rate of freight for cased leather shoes for shipment from Mumbai to London is $600 per 30 cubic feet subject to the availability of space at the vessel.

We maintain sailing at intervals* of approximately 10 days and it takes about 14 days to cover the journey from Mumbai to London. We enclose our sailing time table for the current month and also our shipping instructions* form which you are requested to fill in and return to us duly signed at your earliest.

Yours Faithfully,

×××（Company name）

Sample 3: Customer Advisory — Rate Restoration Program

OOCL Announces Rate Increase on Southeast Asia-Australia Services

Dear Valued Customers,

The ocean freight rates continue to be below the required level to cover basic operating costs or transportation costs in our Southeast Asia-Australia services. Considering that current levels are unsustainable for the long term, we are announcing a rate restoration program for this trade lane*.

In order to maintain a high standard service level and a comprehensive liner network, please be advised that with effect from August 1, freight rates for traffic from Southeast Asia (Singapore, Thailand, Indonesia, Vietnam, Cambodia, Philippines, Indian Subcontinent, Myanmar and Middle East) to Australia will be increased by $200/TEU and $400/FEU for both dry and refrigerated cargo in the base ocean freight. This increase will apply on top of existing ongoing market rates and will be

---

interval
n. 间隔

shipping instruction
装运指示

trade lane
航线

subject to accessorial* surcharges applicable at the time of shipment.

For further information, please kindly contact our local sales representatives.

Thank you for your understanding and continued support.

Yours faithfully,

OOCL

Sample 4: Customer Advisory — General Rate Increase

United States to Middle East General Rate Increase

Dear Valued Customers,

Safmarine will implement a General Rate Increase* for dry shipments going from the United States to the Middle East with an effective date of August 1, 2013.

Please see below for scopes and GRI amounts:

United States to Middle East:

- USD 80 per 20' container
- USD 100 per 40' container
- USD 100 per 45' container

We thank you for your business and look forward to continually serving your global transportation needs.

Sincerely,

Safmarine

Sample 5: Customer Advisory — Bunker Surcharge Adjustment

Bunker Surcharge Adjustment

South East Asia, Middle East, Sub-Continent to Australia

The regular review of bunker costs has been completed and there are changes to the bunker surcharge which are reflected in the table

---

accessorial
adj. 附属的，增加的，补充的

general rate increase
运价上调

below.

Areas and Direction	Cargo Type	20' container	40' container	Effective Date
from: South East Asia, Middle East, Sub-Continent to: Australia	General & Reefer	US＄315	US＄630	11th July, 2012

The new BAF tariff will be applied based on shipment laden onboard date.

The above adjustment has been made from current level of USD 370 per teu, which will expire on 10th July 2012.

For further information visit our local website OOCL－Australia Trade for these and Other surcharges. If this page is useful to you, do bookmark for easy future reference.

Part C: Situational Dialogue

Scene 1: Inquiry of Vessel Schedule And Freight Rate

扫码听音频

A: Hello, this is the Blackbird Furniture Company. I've learned from the shipping schedule that M. V. STAR is sailing for Sydney, and we have some cargo for shipment.

B: Yes. She will call at Sydney port on about January 12th. Can I know the cargo's name?

A: They are all cupboards.

B: And the weight?

A: They are about 3,900 MT. Would you tell me some particulars of M. V. STAR?

B: Let me see.

   Call sign: AIS

   GR/NRT: 8060/7,200.00 MT

   Draft/Dead weight: 12.00 ft. /7,458.00 MT

G/B: 13,088.00/12,446.00 CBM

Holds/Hatches: 3/3

A: How about the speed?

B: Her average speed is 30 knots. And M. V. STAR will be loading at Berth No. 6 from January 12th to 18th inclusive.

A: What about the freight rate?

B: The freight rate for cupboards is US＄59.37 per ton.

A: We'd like to book two hatches of this vessel.

B: OK, let me check. I'll call you back as soon as possible.

A: Thank you. Bye.

B: You are welcome. Bye.

Scene 2: How about LCL

A: What if my cargo is less than a container load?

B: Then the cargo will be consolidated* according to ports of discharge and nature of cargo at the container freight station until there will be a full container load for shipment.

A: Then it will take time, won't it? And I am worried about...

B: Don't worry. It wouldn't take much time. We will pay more attention to that, and be sure you can get the goods on time.

A: Are the containers temperature-controlled?

B: Yes. They are also watertight and airtight to protect goods from being damaged by heat, water or dampness. The containers can be opened at both ends, so that loading and unloading can be made at the same time.

A: Containerization is faster, safer and more convenient. It can also save a lot of wrapping cost and the cost of freight.

consolidate
v. 拼箱

Part D: Related Documents

Sample 1: Quote Request Form

Quote Request Form
Fill out and fax to: 763.550.9949

Tell Us About Yourself:
Name_____ Company (if applicable) _____
Must include one form of contact for us to send quote to:
Telephone_____ Email_____ Facsimile _____

Tell Us About Your Shipment:
Description of your shipment: _____
Value of your shipment: _____
Ship **FROM** City, State and Zip: _____
Ship **TO** City, State and Zip: _____
Dimensions / weight of each piece: _____
_____

Tell Us What Service(s) You Would Like A Quote For: (Check all that apply)
I would like a quote for Freight Dynamics to package my items. _____
My shipment is sufficiently packaged / crated / palletized and ready to ship. _____
I would like a quote to pick up these items for packaging. _____
I will drop my items off at the packaging company. _____
I would like to get a quote for insuring my shipment valued at $_____. _____
The pick up is a Residence. _____
The delivery is a Residence. _____
Liftgate required at Pick-up. _____ (One piece weighs over 150 lbs.)
Liftgate required at Delivery._____ (One piece weighs over 150 lbs.)

Airfreight
Overnight _____ Two Day _____ Three Day _____ 3 to 5 Day Deferred _____
International Priority _____ International Economy_____

Trucking
LTL (Less than truckload) _____ FTL (Full Truckload) _____ Padded Van line _____
Hold At Terminal Service _____

Ocean
Full Container Load 40' _____ Half Container 20' _____ Less than a container _____

How did you hear about us?   **Questions Comments:**
Google search _____   _____
Yahoo search _____   _____
MSN search _____   _____
DEX Yellowpages _____   _____
Superpages.com _____   _____
Other _____   _____

Cargo Canvassing (揽货) Unit 2

Sample 2: Quotation Sheet

QUOTATION	
Exporter XYZ Exporter 8888 Happy Way, Pullman, WA 99163, U.S. Phone: (509)123-456	
Client ABC Importer 6666 Fortune Way, Heze, Shandong 526850, China Phone: (2342)5842-1253	
Product Description	
Quantity	
Unit Price	
EX-WORKS(EXW) Pullman, Washington, U.S. Quotation	
Export Labeling, Translation and Printing	
Export Packaging	
Charges for Loading onto Trucks	
Insurance to Exit Port	
Charges for Export Documentation	
Certificate of Inspection Fees	
Certificate of Health Fees	
Phytosanitary Certificate Fees	
Shippers Export Declaration Fee	
Certificates of Origin Fees	

(Continued)

Charges for Export License	
Banking Charges for Letter of Credit	
Charges for Freight Forwarder	
Inland Freight to Exit Port	
Ocean Terminal Handling Fees, Unloading Charges, Dock Charges, Forklift Charges	
Other Fees	
Free Alongside Ship (FAS) Port of Seattle, Washington, U.S. Quotation	
Charges for Loading onto Ship	
Other Fees	
Free on Board (FOB) Port of Seattle, Washington, U.S. Quotation	
Charges for Harbor Maintenance	
Ocean Freight	
Other Fees	
Cost and Freight (CFR) Port of Qingdao, Shandong, China Quotation	
Insurance to Entry Port	
Other Fees	
Cost, Insurance and Freight (CIF) Port of Qingdao, Shandong, China Quotation	

Sample 3: Sailing Schedule

Hong Kong/South China—Outbound to North America

Attention: Manual VGM cutoff is 8 working hours earlier than eVGM cutoff

Pacific North West 1(PNW2)

Vessel	VOY	Yantian			ETD	ETA	
		eVGM Cutoff	SI Cutoff	CY Cutoff	Yantian	Seattle	Vancouver
CMA CGM NORMA	015TNE	28 May/ 17：00	27 May/ 09：00	28 May/ 12：00	01 Jun	18 Jun	20 Jun
APL SAVANNAH	017TNE	04 Jun/ 17：00	03 Jun/ 09：00	04 Jun/ 12：00	06 Jun	25 Jun	27 Jun
CMA CGM FIDELIO	019TNE	11 Jun/ 17：00	10 Jun/ 09：00	11 Jun/ 12：00	13 Jun	02 Jun	04 Jun
CMA CGM BUTTERFLY	021TNE	18 Jun/ 17：00	17 Jun/ 09：00	18 Jun/ 12：00	20 Jun	09 Jun	11 Jun
CMA CGM MEDEA	023TNE	25 Jun/ 17：00	24 Jun/ 09：00	25 Jun/ 12：00	27 Jun	16 Jun	18 Jun

Updated on 17—May

The sailing schedules/vessels are subject to change without prior notice.

Exercises

Task 1: Listen to the following text and fill in each blank with one or two appropriate words.

扫码听音频

What is Freight or Tariff Rates

The freight rates for export shipments can be obtained by contacting the carrier directly or the carrier's agent or the freight forwarder or consolidator.

The Tariff

Ocean and air carriers have freight rates published in a rate book called the ___①___ , which gives the rates for different kinds of cargo between specific ___②___ worldwide.

The freight conference publishes its ocean cargo rates, while IATA (International Air Transport Association) publishes the air cargo rates. There is no price ___③___ among members within the conferences and the IATA.

Land (road and rail) carriers also have their tariffs, but the cargo rates are often published independently. Hence, a wider ___④___ of rates are often applied among the competing carriers, especially in the highly competitive road transports.

Applicable Tariff Rates

The freight rate is often influenced by the ⑤ of traffic on a given route. When an exporter contacts the carrier or carrier's agent for the freight rate, the information normally required of an exporter is the kind of cargo and its intended ⑥ . Information such as the ⑦ and total cube of the consignment, the expected ⑧ , and whether the freight will be prepaid or ⑨ may also be required. Then, the carrier or carrier's agent refers to the tariff for the applicable freight rate.

Task 2: Fill in the blanks in the following sentences with the words or phrases given below. Change the form where necessary.

quote	TEU	shipper	tariff	freight rate
applicable	canvass	effect	service contract	General Rate Increase

1. Negotiated freight rate refers to the freight rate agreed upon by the international shipping operator and the _____ or the non-vessel shipping operator.

2. The international shipping operator and the non-vessel shipping operator shall carry out the recorded _____ that has taken effect.

3. The salesman in our company is well trained and has rich _____ experiences.

4. A _____ is a confidential contract between a VOCC and one or more shippers in which the shipper(s) make a cargo commitment, and the carrier makes a rate and service commitment.

5. The Merchant's attention is drawn to the stipulations concerning free storage time and demurrage contained in the Applicable _____ .

6. With effect from May 15 2011, freight rate for the westbound traffic from Asia to the Mediterranean and the Black Sea will be increased by USD 275 per _____ .

7. Please be advised that we will apply a _____ with effect from April 1st 2011.

8. OOCL would like to advise our valued customers that we will apply a General Rate Increase on Trans-Atlantic services with _____ from October 1, 2010.

9. The General Rate Increase will apply westbound and eastbound and be _____ to all container types.

10. The above freight rates _____ are subject to THC, DOC & BAF.

Task 3: Match the terms with the following definitions.

1. tariff rate   8. 协议运价

2. freight quote   9. 燃油附加费

3. GRI
4. sales call
5. outstanding freight
6. customer profile
7. shipping gazette

10. 码头操作费
11. 旺季附加费
12. 航运市场
13. 服务合同
14. 船期表

Task 4: Supply the missing words in the blanks of the following letter. The first letters are given.

Port Congestion Surcharge USWC Imports

Dear Valued Customer,

By now we are sure that you are aware of the ongoing labor difficulties on the US West Coast. The s____①____ (局面) has impacted terminal and vessel operations to the point where normal business is simply not possible to continue, and extraordinary costs are being i____②____ (产生) at every step of cargo movement.

The unfortunate result of this is that we will be forced to t____③____ (扳动) the Port Congestion Surcharge that was filed in 2012 in anticipation of possible labor action. The surcharge will be e____④____ (生效) for all cargo discharging at US West Coast ports on or after November 17, 2014. The surcharge will remain in effect until advised otherwise, and will be a____⑤____ (适用) for all cargo and equipment types.

We remain hopeful that the PMA and ILWU will r____⑥____ (解决) the pending labor issues and that the situation will thereafter quickly return to n____⑦____ (正常), allowing us to withdraw this surcharge.

For reference purposes, the q____⑧____ (金额) of the surcharge is as follows:

Size	Type	Level (USD)
20′	(all types)	$800
40′	(all types)	$1000
45′	(all types)	$1266
53′	(all types)	$1600

We thank you for your u____⑨____ (理解) and patience during this challenging situation, and assure you that we are doing everything in our power to continue to keep your supply chain moving as quickly and efficiently as is possible under the circumstances.

Should you have any questions regarding this s____⑩____（附加费）, please contact your local sales representative.

Best regards,

CMA CGM (America) LLC

Unit 3   Booking Acceptance
（接受订舱）

Part A: Basic Knowledge Concerned

Text 1: How to Book Shipping Space

The exporter can book shipping space with a carrier or carrier's agent directly or through a customs broker or forwarder. In practice, it is not uncommon for the exporter to select a carrier and shipping schedule and let the customs broker or forwarder book the space.

Choosing the Carrier

Unless the importer specifies a carrier, the exporter is free to choose a shipping company or airline which offers a competitive rate and can meet the latest date for shipment. Certain importing countries may prohibit the use of flag vessels of a hostile country and any vessels that would make a stopover in a hostile country en route to their territory.

Worldwide Seaports

Please see *Seaports of the World*. Some port names may be spelled differently, for example, Arkhangelsk in the Russian Federation may appear as Archangels.

The letters after the port names in Australia, Canada and the US represent the state or province where the port is located.

Checking the Ocean Shipping Schedules

In many countries, the ocean shipping schedules* (both outbound and inbound) are published in a major newspaper. In countries where newspapers do not carry shipping schedules, the exporter may contact the carrier, customs broker or forwarder for shipping information. The information is also available from private publishers of shipping schedules.

shipping schedule
船期表

Carrier-Voyage/Flight No.

The phrase "Carrier-Voyage*/Flight No." refers to the name of the carrier and its voyage number (in the case of ocean and land freight) or flight number (in the case of air freight).

voyage
n. 航程，航次

In ocean freight, the name of a carrier usually is preceded by letters

merchant vessel 商船	S/S, SS, S. S. , M/V, MV or M. V. . The S/S, SS or S. S. stands for steamship, while M/V, MV or M. V. for merchant* vessel. The term steamship is still widely used despite the fact that modern ships are not propelled by steam.
ETD 预计离港时间 ETA 预计到港时间	**ETD (ETS) and ETA** When booking shipping space, the exporter should know the ETD* (ETS) and ETA* of the shipment. The term ETD is the estimated or expected time of departure from the port or point of origin; it applies to all modes of transportation. ETD is shipment on or about. The term ETS is the estimated or expected time of sailing from the port of origin; it applies to ocean freight. ETS is sailing on or about. The term ETA is the estimated or expected time of arrival at the port or point of destination; it applies to all modes of transportation.
stopover *n.* 中途停留	**Stopover* En Route to Destination** When booking a shipping space, it is important to verify whether the vessel will stopover in other port(s) to unload and load other cargoes en route to the destination. The stopover in certain ports, particularly congested ones, may extend far beyond the expected time.
verbal booking 口头订舱 dead freight 亏舱	**Verbal Booking of Space and Dead Freight** In many countries, verbal booking* of shipping space is accepted, except for dangerous goods. Sometimes, the space booked is not used and the carrier may levy a charge known as dead freight. The exporter must inform the customs broker or forwarder who booked the space on his/her behalf in advance if the space will not be used, so that other shippers may use the space and to avoid paying the dead freight* charge. **Dangerous Goods** When shipping dangerous goods, a written application for shipping space is required. If a shipping order is issued for dangerous goods, it does not mean that the goods will be accepted for loading on

board. When they arrive at the designated customs delivery (closing) location, the goods, shipping order and Dangerous Goods Note are submitted to the ship's master for approval before customs clearance and loading.

Text 2: Reefer Handling and Booking Checklist

The efficiency and effectiveness of reefer containers to perform their purpose in controlling the internal temperature and atmosphere is largely dependent on the pre-loading conditions of cargo and proper packing* and stowage* to enable the desirable air circulation around and through the cargo inside the container. Improper handling during the reefer loading operation not only affects the performance level of the reefer equipment, but also causes serious damage to both the reefer machine unit and the cargo itself. The following is a reference checklist used for loading operations whilst shipper shall determine the proper approach in consideration of variations in cargo nature/post-harvest practices/cargo packaging/regulations etc.

packing
n. 包装
stowage
n. 积载

Before Loading

- A (Pre-Trip Inspection) PTI of the reefer container should be done to ensure the equipment is in good operating condition.
- Pre-cleaning the container to make sure there is no debris* on or beneath the T-floor.

debris
n. 碎片，残骸

- Check and clean the T-floor to ensure the air channel is clear all the way from the panel to the door and free from debris.
- Pre-treat products appropriately and pack them with sufficient protection.
- Pre-cool* products to reach the desired carriage temperature range.

pre-cool
v. 预冷

  Note: Stuffing* hot products may damage both the equipment and cargo!

stuff
v. 装箱

- Pre-cooling of container is not recommended. The exception is the case in which the cargo loading is performed at a cold facility with a temperature-conditioned loading bay connected to the container. The container may be pre-cooled to the appropriate loading temperature.

During Loading

- Do not keep the reefer unit switched-on while the container doors are open, as this could allow condensation* and moisture to develop, which in turn could induce cargo mold and decay.

- Do not store cargo beyond the end of the T-floor, and ensure there is no blockage* at the end of the T-floor channel.

- Do not load above the loading red-line indicated on the container wall, as this will block the return air flow.

- The total floor surface must be covered to avoid short-circuiting of cold air circulation.

- Load cargo as quick and efficient as possible.

Stowage

Frozen Cargo Stowage

- Stowage design is relatively straightforward. As the frozen cargo should have been appropriately pre-cooled to the desired temperature before loading, air circulation should be aimed at blocking and preventing heat penetrating from outside the container.

- Ensure proper corner support of cartons or pallets, according to their weight and loading pressure.

- The entire floor must be evenly* loaded and covered.

- Arrange cargo in a solid block, leaving no space between the packages/cartons to avoid hotspot* or short-circuit*.

- Stowage must not exceed the red-line to avoid air circulation blockage. The aim is to allow air circulation "around" the entire cargo load.

- Ventilation and dehumidification must be set to "Off". Drain port must be "Closed".

Chilled Cargo Stowage

- Stowage is designed to allow proper air circulation and flow-through of the entire cargo load so that heat, vapor, CO_2, and other gases produced by the respiration process from chilled

---

condensation
n. 冷凝，凝结

blockage
n. 堵塞

evenly
adv. 均匀地，平衡地

hotspot
n. 热点，热区

short-circuit
n. 短路

perishable* products can be removed.

- Proper air passages should be present on the packaging, with particular attention to the size, number, and position of vent holes on cartons, to allow refrigerated air to circulate through all the cargo in the container.

- Proper packaging (for example, packaging style, package material, and so forth) must be used to support stacking weight and sustainability at various humidity levels.

- Shrink-wrap*, slip-sheet, foam trays, plastic bags, and so forth that block or obstruct air passage should not be used.

- If cargo cannot cover entire floor, cardboard can be used to cover empty spaces to avoid short circuit of the refrigerated airflow.

- There must be no stowage above the indicated red line on the container walls to avoid impeding return air flow.

Booking Information Checklist

Customers should provide the following critical shipment information:

- Specific Origin and Destination.
- A detailed description of the product(s) being shipped, e.g. commodity, quantity, weight, cubic measurement, and type of packaging (boxed, drums, pallets*, hanging carcass, and so forth).
- Preferred equipment size (20′ or 40′HC).
- Preferred temperature set-point (specify in °F or °C).
- Fresh-air exchange requirements (specify in CFM or CMH).
- Modified or controlled atmosphere requirements.
- The date when the product is available at the point of origin and the required delivery date at the destination.
- Special handling requirements (e.g. dehumidification % level, Cold Treatment, and so forth).
- If container pre-cooling is required, the booking office should be informed.

---

perishable
adj. 易腐烂的

shrink-wrap
n. 包装用的收缩胶膜

pallet
n. 托盘，货板

Part B: Business Letters

Sample 1: Enquiry Letter Regarding the Sailings and Freight Rate

Dear Sirs,

We shall be glad to have a schedule of your sailings to _____ (place name), _____ (date) and the freight rates for cases 25cm×1cm×50cm each weighing _____ (amount) kg.

Also please let us know the usual time taken for the voyage.

Thank you.

Yours faithfully,

(Company Manager Name)

Sample 2: Reply to Above

Dear Sir,

We thank you for your letter of _____ and have pleasure in enclosing a schedule of our sailings during the next quarter. The freight rate for your cases will be _____ (amount) per case. The voyage to _____ (place name) takes _____ (number of days). The goods will have to be delivered at our above address and in case you wish us to collect the same from your factory, an expense of _____ (amount) per case will be charged subject to a minimum of _____ (amount).

We are enclosing our shipping form and shall be glad to hear further.

Thank you.

Yours faithfully,

(Company Name)

Sample 3: Customer Advisory — Service Enhancement

Dear Valued Customer,

To enhance our service coverage in the Asia-North Europe trade, we are pleased to inform you that our Loop 6 product will add westbound calls to Fuzhou and Nansha with the following details:

New port rotation: Fuzhou — Kaohsiung — Xiamen — Nansha — Shekou — Hong Kong — Singapore — Colombo — Southampton — Antwerp — Hamburg — Rotterdam — Jebel Ali — Shekou — Fuzhou.

Effective voyage: APL Le Havre (LHV) 016 W with Kaohsiung ETA on July 24, 2015.

For further information, please kindly contact our local representatives or find out the latest sailing schedule.

Thank you for your support of OOCL.

With kind regards,

OOCL

Sample 4: New Service Notice

Dear Customer,

We will newly deploy an Asia-Africa service FW3, the first vessel is MAERSK CAIRO Voyage 1201 which is estimated to depart from Shanghai on May 29, 2012. The FW3 service calling Yang Shan phase* I and vessel agent is UNISCO.

phase
n. 阶段，期

Operation deadlines as below:

CY Open:	FRI 1200
Complete MDGF Cutoff:	THU 1300
Booking Close:	FRI 1730
Print E-release Order Application:	SUN 0830
CY Close:	SUN 2300
DR* Cutoff:	SUN 2300
ETA:	MON 1400
ETD:	TUE
Shipping Instruction Cutoff:	SUN 1400

DR, Dock Receipt
场站收据

Rotation* and discharge port coded as below:

　　Qingdao, P. R. C.
　　Shanghai, P. R. C.
　　Nansha, P. R. C

rotation
n. 靠港顺序

Tanjung Pelepas, Malaysia	MYTPP
Cape Town, South Africa	ZACPT
Pointe Noire, Congo	CGPNR
Tema, Ghana	GHTMA

If there are any further changes, we will keep you posted.

Should you have any queries, please do not hesitate to contact our customer service representatives.

Thank you for your ever-lasting support and cooperation.

With kind regards,

Maersk (China) Shipping Co., Ltd. Shanghai Branch

Sample 5: Customer Advisory — Service Omission

Dear Valued Customer,

Please be advised that Hatta, Voyage 107GXE on our Amerigo Mina service will be blanked from USEC* ports for week 4, 2016.

All cargo to Persian Gulf can be booked on Indamex service — OOCL Kobe Voy. 70INE, port cut New York January 18, port cut Norfolk January 20, port cut Savannah January 22.

All cargo to North Africa, East Africa & West Africa can be advanced to Al Rawdah Voy. 99GXE and CMA CGM Racine Voy. 103GXE.

Amerigo line schedule for January 2016:

 Week 1—Buxcoast Voy. 95GXE.
 Week 2—Al RawdahVoy. 99GXE.
 Week 3—CMA CGM Racine Voy. 103GXE.
 Week 4—Blank sailing.
 Week 5—Al Bahia Voy. 111GXE.

Thank you for your continued support. Should you have any questions or concerns regarding this change, please contact your local CMA CGM sales representative. For current schedule activity, please visit our web site at *www.cma-cgm.com*.

Best regards,

USEC
美国东海岸

CMA CGM (America) LLC

Part C: Situational Dialogue

扫码听音频

Scene 1: Talking About Export Documents for Chemical Cargo.

A: Hello, may I speak to Johnny?

B: Yes, this is Johnny speaking.

A: Have you received my FCL* booking to New York sent yesterday?

B: Yes, I am preparing the quotation* and will send it to you soon. But I need to check the handling with you at first because it's chemical cargo.

A: Yes, the commodity is cartridge used in laser printers.

B: Okay, no problem. Thus please prepare the MSDS* document and I will send you a guarantee letter sample. Please add the cargo details on the letter based on the sample. And please send us the original documents with your company's chop. Without above documents, carriers won't release the space to you.

A: I got it! I will prepare the documents as well as other export documents for you.

B: Oh, you have to send the MSDS document to us in advance to confirm the space with the carrier. The export documents can be sent to us later after the space is released and the CY closing time is confirmed from the terminal.

A: Okay, I will prepare soon and send them out today. And I will ask our factory to finish producing goods in time.

B: Thank you very much for your assistance. Do you need us to do container stuffing at your factory or at our warehouse?

A: Please prepare container haulage at our factory. Please don't forget to quote me the haulage fee together with ocean freight.

B: Sure. I will inform you of that once the space is confirmed, and I'll check the container stuffing time with you.

A: Thank you!

FCL
整箱货
quotation
n. 报价

MSDS
化学品安全说明书

— 47 —

Scene 2: How to Deal with a Complaining Customer.

A: Do you know how to deal with a complaining customer?

B: No matter by what way, don't get angry with it. It is better to communicate with a complaining customer. Using the following steps to help you handle and solve the problem.

A: What is your suggestion?

B: First of all, you should listen and take notes. Write down any names, dates, and major points of complaint.

A: Well, I agree with you, and go on.

B: Secondly, think twice before making promises. Express your regret for his or her dissatisfaction and any inconvenience he or she may have experienced, but think before you give any promise — because nothing annoys customers more than a broken promise*.

A: That is the exact question.

B: Thirdly, check the facts. Make sure the information the customer has given you is correct and work out solutions by yourself.

A: Yes, to respect the facts is the basis. What should to do next?

B: The last step is to offer solutions. When the customer complains, you should always offer him a solution to the problem. If you cannot directly fix the problem, offer him something else to try and keep him satisfied.

A: What does the customer service do to solve various problems?

B: There are many different types of solutions which could turn a disappointed customer into a happy one, such as, to offer a replacement, refund the money*, offer a repair, offer a discount on the next purchase, and apologize for the inconvenience caused.

broken promise
违约

refund the money
退钱

Part D: Related Documents

Sample 1: Booking Note

华南区订仓及拖车联系单

BOOKING NO:

Booking Party(Full Name & Address) 订舱公司名称和地址:	Shipper(Full Name & Address) 付货人名称和地址:
Contact Person 联络人: Tel 电话: Email Address 电子邮件: Fax 传真:	Contact Person 联络人: Tel 电话: Email Address 电子邮件: Fax 传真:
Consignee(Full Name & Address) 收货人名称和地址:	Notify Party (Full Name & Address) 通知人名称和地址:

Service Contract No.合约号:	运费付款安排:	Freight Prepaid 预付 [ ] Freight Collect 到付 [ ]	
Intended Vessel/Voyage 船名/航次:	Place of Receipt 收货地:	Port of Loading 装货港:	Port of Discharging 卸货港:	Place of Delivery 目的地:

| Sizes & Numbers of Container: 柜型& 柜数
 20GP( )   40GP( )   40HQ( )
 45HQ( )   20RF( )   40RQ( ) | Description of Goods 货名 | Gross Weight (Ton) 毛重(吨) | Measurement 立方米 |

[ ] Dangerous Cargo 险货,请填货物包装证明书   [ ] Hanging Garment Cargo 挂衣柜,请填挂衣表格
[ ] Reefer Cargo 冻柜,请填冻柜联系单
美国进口清关地点: [ ] Local Port Customs Clearance 港口清关   [ ] Inland Customs Clearance 内陆清关
是否委托OOCL办理<集装箱检验检疫结果单>是 [ ] 否 [ ]

1. 拖车及报关方式:
1.1 委托OOCL拖车 [ ] 是   (请详细提供以下资料及提早一个工作日预约拖车)
        货柜数量及类型: _____ 到厂日期及时间: _____
        工厂/仓库名称
        及装货地点: _____
        装货联络人: _____ 电话: _____
1.2 自行拖车   [ ] 是   备注: _____

2. 报关方式:
2.1 委托OOCL代报关
    [ ] 是   [ ] 转关   转关地点(客人必须自行在当地封关)   联络人及电话: _____
            [ ] 清关   (客人必须在截柜前三日将所有报关文件交到以下报关行)

盐田出口	公司:深圳市外代报关有限公司 地址:深圳盐田港海港大厦815室	联络人:张小姐/王小姐 电话:755-xxxxxx
蛇口及赤湾出口	公司:深圳市天晟国际货运有限公司 地址:深圳市南山区前海湾临海路海运中心主塔楼313室	联络人:钟小姐/李小姐 电话:755-xxxxxx
其它地区	请联络当地的客户服务部	

2.2 自行报关   [ ] 是   备注: _____

3. 其他方式:
港口建设费的付款方式:是否委托OOCL代交予船代: 是 [ ]   否 [ ] ===> 客人需自行交予码头
港口设施保安费的付款方式:是否委托OOCL代交予码头: 是 [ ]   否 [ ] ===> 客人需自行交予码头
经中港拖车的港口设施保安费的付款方式:是否委托OOCL代交予码头: 是 [ ] 否 [ ]===>客人需提供电子代用券副本,或代用券正本或预先申报编号.

4. 注意事项:
4.1 如欲取消已订之舱柜,请于出车前一个工作天通知本公司,否则由此产生之额外费用由托运人支付。
4.2 委托拖车截止时间: 到厂日期前一天16:00 [星期一至五], 11:30 [星期六]。
4.3 货物在拖运期间,若有额外费用产生 (如:报关、查车、消毒检疫及压车、压架、关塞费用等) 均由客户负责。

Booking Party's Signature and Company Chop

Sample 2: Booking Confirmation

BOOKING CONFIRMATION

Booking No.: **580302807**   打印时间:2016-12-05 09:12 UTC

订舱人:	SINOTRANS EASTERN CO LTD SHIPPING	交接方式:	CY/CY
联系人:	PAC CONFIRM	收货地:	Shanghai,Shanghai,China
订舱人参考号:		交货地:	Charleston,South Carolina,United States
合约号:		客人提供货物描述:	in gauge-MIRROR
合约客户:	TOPOCEAN CONSOLIDATION SERVICE INC	受理订舱分公司:	Maersk China Shipping (East China)
参考号:		Shipper Ref. No:	

We thank you for your booking and enclose your booking details as follows :-

Kindly note that we are applying container.

集装箱信息

数量	尺寸/箱型/ 高度	(英尺.英是否可折叠)	替代箱型	货物总重量	包装数量/种类	货物体积
1	20 OPEN	8 6		18490.000 KGS	10 Piece(s)	20.0000

预期运输计划

出发	到达	船名	航次	预计出发日期	预计到达日期
Yangshan, SGH Shengdong Terminal	Charleston Terminal N598	MAERSK UTAH	650E	2016-12-19	2017-01-17

提箱还箱指引

Type	Location	Release Date	From	To	Return Date	Time	Load Ref.
Empty Container Depot	Shanghai Dewell Cont. Trans.co. LTD Shanghai Dewell Cont. Trans.co. LTD No. 1568 Gangcheng road Shanghai	2016-12-05	06:01				
Return Equip Delivery Terminal	Yangshan, SGH Shengdong Terminal Yangshan, SGH Shengdong Terminal 1299 Ganghua Road Pudong New Area Shanghai						

为避免混淆，现解释我司相关订舱文件区别如下。本文件种类请参见右上角英文标题。
BOOKING CONFIRMATION - 订舱确认单，兹证明我公司已确认客户订舱。
BOOKING AMENDMENT - 订舱确认单更改件，兹证明原订舱确认单的内容已作修改。
BOOKING ACKNOWLEDGEMENT - 订舱单回执，谨证明我司已收到客户的订舱单，但该订舱尚未确认，相关信息请以订舱确认单为准。
BOOKING CANCELLATION - 订舱取消单，兹证明客户订舱单已被取消。

拖箱指示:
pending for container

This document is subject to following:
-This booking and carriage are subject to the Maersk Line Terms and Conditions of Carriage which are available upon request from the carrier or his representatives and are furthermore accessible on the Maersk Line website "<http://www.maerskline.com>" under "Services" / "General Business Terms".
-The shipment is subject to tariff rates unless a correct and applicable service contract number is available
-The carrier's right to substitute the named and/or performing vessel(s) with another vessel or vessels at any time.
-Arrival, berthing, departure and transit times are estimated and given without guarantee and subject to change without prior notice
-All dates/times are given as reasonable estimates only and subject to change without prior notice.
Shipments destined for or carried/transhipped via the USA:
- This document is given subject to the customer providing the correct cargo description in accordance with U.S. law, including U.S. Customs requirements as described in Customs Rules and Regulations, 19 CFR Parts 4, 113 and 178 of October 31, 2002

Booking Acceptance
（接受订舱） Unit 3

BOOKING CONFIRMATION

Booking No.:	MCT632594	**Print Date:**	2017-03-21 03:30 UTC
Booked by Party:	CHINATRANS INTL LTD GZ	**Service Mode:**	CY/CY
Contact Name:	XUE LYRIC	**From:**	Yantian,Guangdong,China
Booked by Ref. No:		**To:**	Chittagong,Bangladesh
Price Owner:	MCC RATE SHEET	**Customer Cargo:**	
Ref. No:		**Business Unit:**	MCC China (Guangzhou)
Service Contract:	293678377	**Shipper Ref. No:**	

Equipment

Quantity	Size/Type/Height (ft.in) Collapsible	Sub. Equip	Gross Weight	Pack. Qty/Kind	Cargo Volume
1	20 DRY 8 6		5000.000 KGS		

Intended Transport Plan

From	To	Mode	Vessel	Voy No.	ETD	ETA
YanTian Intl. Container Terminal	Chittagong Terminal	MVS	CAPE SYROS	1707	2017-03-26	2017-04-04

Load Itinerary

Type	Location	Release From Date	Time	Release To Date	Time	Return Date	Time	Load Ref.
Empty Container Depot	YanTian Intl. Container Terminal YanTian Intl. Container Terminal YanTian Terminal Yantian	2017-03-21	01:00					
Return Equip Delivery Terminal	YanTian Intl. Container Terminal YanTian Intl. Container Terminal YanTian Terminal Yantian							

Service: IA7 SB INTENDED TRANSPORT PLAN FOR REFERENCE ONLY AND SUBJECT TO CHANGE(CAPE SYROS).
CY Closing: Saturday, Mar 25, 2017 16:00
VGM Submission Deadline: E Channel 25/Mar/2017 20:00:00 Non E-Channel 25/Mar/2017 16:00:00
Voucher Cut Off: Saturday, Mar 25, 2017 18:00
SI Cut Off: Friday, Mar 24, 2017 20:00
CY Open Date: Monday, Mar 20, 2017 00:00
20'DC/40'DC 28TON PAYLOAD EQU: NO
Special Remarks: None

1. Booking: Please place the new booking via WWW.MCC.COM.SG . If you want to revise/cancel booking, please email to public email of customer service desk.
2. Please submit your shipping instructions (SI) on time via www.mcc.com.sg ; Amendments after SI submission are subject to an amendment fee of RMB300/HKD450 per BL per time.
3. Payment: Please send debit note request to: (pay at Guangzhou)GUAFINPMTGEN@MAERSK.COM; (pay at HKG)HKGFINPMTGEN@MAERSK.COM; (pay at Shenzhen)SZHFINPMTGEN@MAERSK.COM once vessel departures. Please arrange payment within 10 calendar days.
4. OTHERS: For more information please visit www.mcc.com.sg
5. Heavy Weight Surcharge is subject to actual cargo weight. The 'Equipment Pickup Date' in the booking confirmation is for reference only. Please refer to CY OPEN/CY CLOSING to arrange empty pickup.
Customer Service Contact :   CN.SOUTH.EXPORT@MCC.COM.SG
Yantian Penavico address: 8/F Floor Harbour Building Yantian Port Shenzhen 深圳市盐田港海港大厦主楼 8 楼

This booking is subject to following:
- Space and equipment availability
- The carrier reserves the right to substitute the named and/or performing vessel(s) with another vessel or vessels at any time
- Arrival, berthing, departure and transit times are estimated and given without guarantee and subject to change without prior notice
- All dates/times are given as reasonable estimates only and subject to changes
- This booking and carriage are subject to the MCC TRANSPORT terms and Conditions of Carriage which are available upon request from the carrier on his representatives and are furthermore accessible on the MCC website <http://www.mcc.com.sg>" under "terms of carriage".
- The Merchant shall ensure that cargo weight doesn't exceed the max payload of the container, and shall comply with all regulations or requirements of customs, port and other authorities, and shall bear and pay all duties, taxes, fines, imposts, expenses or losses (including, without prejudice to the generality of the foregoing Freight for any additional Carriage undertaken), incurred or suffered by reason thereof, or by reason of any illegal, incorrect or insufficient declaration or by reason of any illegal, incorrect or insufficient declaration of weight and measurements, marking, numbering or addressing of the Goods, and shall indemnify the Carrier in respect thereof.

Exercises

Task 1: Listen to the following text and fill in each blank with one or two appropriate words.

An enquiry in shipping business is a request for information on shipping space, freight rates, ___①___ of sailing, charter hire, and other shipping services. A shipper may send out an enquiry to a shipping company or an agent inviting a ___②___ or tariff for the goods to be shipped. A foreign-trade firm may inquire of a ship owner or broker about chartering a ship. Enquiries can be made by letter, fax or even telephone.

When writing a letter of inquiry, you should observe the following rules.

1. Begin with the sentence by introducing yourself or your company and state directly the ___③___ of your inquiry.

2. For each item of information you want, use a ___④___ paragraph.

3. Keep your enquiry brief, ___⑤___ and to the point; say what needs to be said, ask what needs to be asked and no more.

Since enquiries represent a great ___⑥___ of business, the answers to enquiries should be ___⑦___, courteous and helpful. When writing a reply, you should first thank the enquirer for his/her enquiry, mention the date of his/her letter and quote any other references that appear. Give the information fully and efficiently the enquirer has asked for. Finally express the hope of a ___⑧___ friendly business relationship so as to create ___⑨___ and leave good impression on the customer.

Task 2: Fill in the blanks in the following sentences with the words or phrases given below. Change the form where necessary.

sailing schedule	port rotation	shipping order	transit time	subject
carrier	shipping space	frequency	unbalanced	ETA

1. The sailing schedules are _____ to change without prior notice.

2. When booking, the shipper should know the ETD (ETS) and _____ of the shipment.

3. The _____ number will not be released unless full booking information has been received.

4. We are booking _____ for the shipment.

5. We will select the _____ and advise you of the carrier's shipping order number.

6. Our _____ to Tokyo and Kobe is currently fixed on every Monday and Friday. As for Pusan, it falls on every Sunday.

7. Please be advised that CPX service will change _____ effect from May 2012.

8. Hapag-Lloyd will continue to provide you with a comprehensive product including multiple weekly sailings and attractive _____ to serve your transportation needs.

9. A container liner shipping network operated by a particular shipping line comprises a set of ship routes with given service _____ and strings of homogenous ships in terms of capacity and average sailing speed.

10. The world trade is _____: the volume of export containers at a port can be significantly different from that of import containers.

Task 3: Translate the following terms.

1. booking note   6. 运输时间
2. booking confirmation   7. 订舱人
3. sailing schedule   8. 舱位
4. port rotation   9. 装运单
5. ETD/ETA   10. 货物接收地

Task 4: Supply the missing words in the blanks of the following letter. The first letters are given.

Customer advisory: Vessel Phase-out Plan

Dear Customer,

Please be a _____①_____ (通知) that the vessel CMA CGM BELLINI V: 7119 will be phased out in Singapore and r _____②_____ (替换) by PERFORMANCE V: 7119.

Consequently all cargo b _____③_____ (预订) on vessel CMA CGM BELLINI V: 7119 will be t _____④_____ (转移) to vessel PERFORMANCE V: 7119.

Vessel details:

    Vessel Name   PERFORMANCE
    Vessel IMO   9250971
    Year Built   2002
    Flag   MALTA

Should you have any inquiries, please do not h _____⑤_____ (犹豫) to contact the CMA CGM customer service team on one of the following numbers.

Export Cargo 1800 188 129

Import Cargo 1800 187 928

Sincerely,

CMA-CGM

Unit 4　Empty Container Release
（发放空箱）

Empty Container Release
（发放空箱） Unit 4

Part A: Basic Knowledge Concerned

Text 1: What Do the Markings on a Container Mean?

Everyone may have seen the markings on a container, especially the door when it comes to the warehouse for packing or unpacking.

Each of these markings plays a very significant role in the transportation of the container and provides vital information to all entities in the supply chain relating to the monitoring and safety of the container and cargo during its carriage.

Let us look at each of these markings individually based on the image below showing the various markings.

Container Number

Container number is of course the main marking on the door. It is an alpha numeric sequence made up of 4 alphabets and 7 numbers.

The container number identification system has been created by the International Standards Organization under their code ISO 6346: 1995(E).

As per this code, the container identification system consists of:

owner code
箱主代码

- Owner code* — 3 letters (in above example, HLX).
- Equipment category — 1 letter (in above example, U denoting a freight container. Other categories being J for detachable container related equipment, such as Genset, and Z for trailers and chassis).

serial number
序列号

check digit
校验码

- Serial number* — 6 numbers (numbers ONLY).
- Check Digit* — 1 number (numbers ONLY).

The owner code is UNIQUE to the owner of the container and the registration of this code rests with Bureau International des Containers et du Transport Intermodal (BIC). This is to avoid any duplication of code by any shipping line or container operator.

If you don't know who a particular container belongs to, you can always do a BIC Code Search to identify the owner of the container.

lease
v. 租赁

But BEWARE, the owner of the container need not necessarily be operating the container as they could have leased* the container to another operator or shipping line.

Check Digit

Although it is part of the full container number, the check digit is a VERY IMPORTANT number as it can be used to identify if the above mentioned identification sequence is valid or invalid.

For example, if you go to BIC's Check Digit Calculator and type in the prefix — HLXU and the numbers 200841, see what you get as the Check Digit.

Container Owner or Lessor

This is the entity that owns or operates the container. This could be a shipping line, like in this example (Hapag Lloyd) or a container leasing company such as Textainer whose business is to lease containers to shipping lines that need to increase their inventory but not their assets.

max gross
最大总重量

SOLAS
海上人命安全公约

VGM
核实的集装总重

Max Gross*

In this example, 30,480 kg is the maximum weight that the container can carry including its own tare weight of 2,250 kg.

This is the weight that the SOLAS* VGM* Certificate must show.

Empty Container Release (发放空箱) Unit 4

ISO Code

As per the International Standards Organization under their code ISO 6346: 1995(E), each container is given a unique ISO Code in order to avoid any ambiguity* in naming the container.

For example, a standard 20' container is called Dry Van (DV)/General Purpose (GP)/Standard (SD)/Normal, Dry Container (DC)/etc. in different countries.

As these terms are all different, these terms cannot be used in uniform systems that are used for transmission of data across ports, customs, shipping lines etc. Therefore as a standard, the ISO code of 22G1 (in the above example) is used to denote that the container in question is a 20' container 8'6" high with a tare weight of 2,250 kg.

Classification Society Label for Type Testing

Each container is tested for its strength, cargo and seaworthiness by a classification society and this label indicates which classification society certified* this box.

Tare Weight*

This is the actual weight of an empty container and this is given by the manufacturer at the end of the manufacturing and labeling process. This is an important weight to be considered by all ship operators and planners as this weight needs to be included when planning the ship and SHOULD NOT BE IGNORED by the planners.

Imagine the mega ships which carry around 19,000 TEUs. If the tare of each TEU (2,250 kg) is ignored, the ship will have an unaccounted weight of 42,750,000 kg=42,750 t. That is asking for a disaster at sea.

However, this weight is also heavily contested by the trade and shipping lines in terms of whether this weight should be shown on the Bill of Lading or not, and whether the VGM weight should match the Bill of Lading weight or not.

Max. Payload*

This is the maximum weight of the cargo that can be packed in the container and the mis-declaration of this weight by the customers

---

ambiguity
n. 含糊

certify
v. 认证
tare weight
皮重, 箱子自重

payload
n. 载重量

has severe consequences both to life and property.

This is the weight that is shown on the Bill of Lading and to reconfirm, it DOES NOT INCLUDE THE TARE WEIGHT OF THE CONTAINER.

This weight is clearly shown on the door of the container and customers cannot feign ignorance that they were not aware of the capacity of the container.

Cube

This is the maximum volume in cubic capacity that can be packed into the container. Unlike weight, it is not possible to overpack the container by volume as it will be quite evident.

While (unlike mis-declaration of weight) mis-declaration of volume may not have any physical consequence, mis-declaration of volume on a Bill of Lading could have some financial consequences for the buyer or seller especially if the cargo is sold by volume.

CSC*, ACEP & Other Certifications

CSC 国际集装箱安全公约

Every container should have a valid safety approval plate called CSC (Container Safety Convention) plate in order for it to be used in international trade. This is in accordance with the provisions of the International Convention on Safe Containers of 1972.

The role of this CSC plate is to confirm that the container has been inspected and found to be in a condition suitable for transportation on board the ship.

This plate has all the details of the Owners, Technical Data, and ACEP* information (ACEP being short for Approved Continuous Examination Programme). In short, every 30 months a container must be turned into a Container Depot for examination.

ACEP 集装箱安全连续检验计划

Other than the above mentioned markings, containers also have other markings such as:

1. The full container number.

- On the roof of the container—for the benefit of crane operators during loading/unloading operations.

- Inside the container close to the door—for the benefit of the packing people/surveyors etc..

Empty Container Release
(发放空箱) Unit 4

- On the back of the container — for the benefit of transporters/government authorities/etc. during transportation as it is normal to transport the container with the doors facing the inside of the truck for security purposes.

2. Indicators for fork lift pockets for the benefit for fork lift operators.

3. Caution stickers on 40'/45' High Cube containers indicating that it is a high container.

Text 2: Equipment Control Guidance

Empty Container Reservation

1. Pay EIR* fee & print EIR (include EIR for picking up empty & returning full) via web *http://eir.cmclink.com* after receiving CMA booking confirmation.

> EIR
> 设备交接单

2. Send SMS for empty reservation one working day before pick up empty, SMS will reply with the empty picking-up location.

3. Pick up empty from the assigned location. Depot*/terminal will release empty against EIR & EDI data.

> depot
> n. 堆场

4. Return full to terminal before CY closing. Terminal will accept full gate in against EIR & EDI data.

Empty Return After Empty Pick Up

1. Pay D&D charge/lifting charge/EIR fee in CMA terminal Office. CMA terminal office will issue the EIR when D&D charge/EIR fee/lifting charge is paid. The location and the valid date for empty return, will be shown in the EIR.

- Lifting*: two lifting shall be charged, including one for empty out & one for empty return.

> lifting
> n. 吊次

- D&D: charged from empty picking up date to empty return date, no free day.

2. Return empty to the assigned depot within valid date shown on EIR. Depot will inspect the empty before accept it, and the client shall pay the repair charge (if any) to the depot on site.

Export Full Withdrawing*, then Empty/Full Return

> withdraw
> n. 退场

1. Pay D&D charge/lifting charge/EIR fee in CMA terminal

Office. After getting cargo release confirmation from CMA CUS dept., CMA terminal office will issue the EIR when D&D charge/lifting charge/EIR fee is paid. The valid date (for picking up full & container return) and the location for container return, will be shown in the EIR.

- Lifting: four lifting shall be charged for empty return, and three lifting shall be charged for full return.

- D&D: charged from empty picking up date to empty return date for empty return, no free day, and charged from empty pick up date to full pick up date for full return, no free day.

2. Pick up full from terminal. Terminal will collect storage, electricity fee or other terminal fee if any, and then release full against EIR & Customs Releasing Voucher.

3. Return the devanning* empty to the assigned depot within valid date shown on EIR. Depot will inspect the devanning empty before accept it, and the client shall pay the repair charge (if any) to the depot on site.

4. Pay EIR fee in CMA terminal office. CMA will issue the EIR for full return when EIR fee is paid.

5. Return full to terminal before CY closing. Terminal will accept full gate in against EIR & EDI data.

Pick Up Inbound Full & Devanning Empty Return

1. Pay D&D charge/EIR fee in CMA terminal Office. After getting cargo release confirmation from CMA CUS & Finance dept., CMA terminal office will issue the EIR when D&D charge/EIR fee is paid. The valid date (for picking up full & empty return) and the location for empty return, will be shown in the EIR.

2. Pick up full from terminal within the valid date shown on EIR. Terminal will collect storage, electricity fee or other terminal fee if any, and then release full against the EIR & Customs Release Voucher.

3. Return the devanning empty to the assigned depot within valid date shown on EIR. Depot will inspect the devanning empty before accept it, and the client shall pay the repair charge (if any) to the depot on site.

---

devanning
adj. 已拆箱的

Empty Container Release
(发放空箱) Unit 4

Part B: Business Letters

Sample 1: Empty Container Pick Up*/Drop Off* Charges

pick up
提箱
drop off
还箱

Dear Valued Customers,

Please be informed about the implementation of a pick-up/drop-off charge for the pick-up/drop-off of an empty container at a depot at Hamburg or Bremerhaven in case the load/discharge port for that shipment is not the same (Example: Pick-up at Hamburg and load port Bremerhaven).

This charge is implemented in view of the increasing demand of empty container positioning. It shall also contribute to safeguard the availability of empty equipment for our customers in future.

Effective date will be: 1st March 2016 (Booking date).

Quantum will be: EUR 50,00 per Standard Container.

      EUR 75,00 per Special Equipment Container.

The prevailing cost structure at Inland depots is not affected by this charge and remains unchanged.

For further information, please contact your local MSC office.

Best regards,
MSC

Sample 2: Advisory of Shanghai Export Empty Container Yangshan Pick Up

Dear Valued Customers,

To serve your export empty container pick up in a better way, with effective as from 14th July 2014, Maersk Line will further develop empty pick up at Yangshan Guandong terminal. Furthermore, customers can enjoy 3 days early pick up at Yangshan, which means empty pick up 10 days prior to vessel departure (including vessel ETD). For non-Yangshan pick up, we open empty container pick up 7 days prior to vessel departure (including vessel ETD). Please ensure to refer to empty release order to arrange the trucking.

We thank you for your always support for Safmarine. Should you have further queries, please feel free to contact your local Safmarine representative.

With regards,

Safmarine

Sample 3: Customer Advisory — Shanghai Port Congestion*

congestion
n. 拥堵

Dear Customer,

The port of Shanghai is currently facing serious congestion. The schedules of several services have been impacted and vessel operations are experiencing a delay of multiple days.

The congestion is mainly attributable to bad weather (fog) and some issues relating to the transition to new alliances.

NYK is monitoring the situation and cooperating with the port authority very closely to ensure that normal terminal operations and schedule integrity are recovered as soon as possible.

In the interim we will continue to regularly refresh schedule information in line with operational developments.

There is a public announcement from the Shanghai International Port Group available at *www.portshanghai.com.cn*.

Please contact your NYK Line representative should you have any further questions.

Yours faithfully,

NYK Line (China) Co. Ltd.

Part C: Situational Dialogue

扫码听音频

Scene: Container Trucking Arrangement

A: Can you deliver a shipping container to my area?

B: Yes, we can deliver shipping containers to most areas in southern China.

A: What is the cost for delivery?

B: You will need to provide us with your zip code or town so we can give you accurate quote on storage containers and delivery as our prices vary at different ports and cities.

A: What is the size of a standard shipping container?

B: If you visit our container dimension page, you will find the specifications including weight and height on all sizes of cargo containers.

A: What form of payment do you accept?

B: We accept all major credit/debit cards, bank wire transfers.

A: What is the condition of a used container?

B: All of our used shipping containers are guaranteed wind, watertight* and lockable* in excellent condition. All shipping containers can be seaworthy inspected and certified by us to be used for overseas shipping.

A: Can I use these containers to ship overseas?

B: Yes, All of our used cargo containers are seaworthy*/cargo worthy*. Contact us to have your shipping container inspected and certified for shipping before delivery.

A: Do I need a permit from my town to have a container at my residence or business?

B: No, Storage containers are not considered a permanent structure and are portable. No special permits are required.

A: What type of foundation do I need to place a container on?

B: Any flat solid foundation is suitable.

A: Thank you for your information.

B: You are welcome. Contact us with any other questions you may have.

---

watertight
adj. 防水的

lockable
adj. 可锁定的，可封闭的

seaworthy
adj. 适航的

cargo worthy
adj. 适货的

Part D: Shipping Documents

Sample: Equipment Interchange Receipt

集装箱发放/设备交接单

EQUIPMENT INTERCHANGE RECEIPT   NO:

用箱人/运箱人(CONTAINER USER/HAULIER)	提箱地点(PLACE OF DELIVERY)
发往地点(DELIVERED TO)	返回/收箱地点(PLACE OF RETURN)

航名/航次(VESSEL/VOYAGE NO.)	集装箱号(CONTAINER NO.)	尺寸/类型(SIZE/TYPE)	营运人(CNTR. OPTR.)

提单号(B/L NO.)	铅封号(SEAL NO.)	免费期限(FREE TIME PERIOD)	运载工具牌号 (TRUCK WAGON. BARGE NO.)

出场目的/状态(PPS OF GATE-OUT/STATUS)	进场目的/状态(PPS OF GATE-IN/STAUS)	出场日期(TIME-OUT)
		月　日　时

出场检查记录 (INSPECTION AT THE TIME OF INTERCHANGE)

普通集装箱 (GP CONTAINER)	冷藏集装箱 (RF CONTAINER)	特种集装箱 (SPECIAL CONTAINER)	发电机 (GEN SET)
☐ 正常(SOUND)	☐ 正常(SOUND)	☐ 正常(SOUND)	☐ 正常(SOUND)
☐ 异常(DEFECTIVE)	☐ 异常(DEFECTIVE)	☐ 异常(DEFECTIVE)	☐ 异常(DEFECTIVE)

损坏记录及代号(DAMAGE & CODE)　　BR 破损(BROKEN)　　D 凹损(DENT)　　M 丢失(MISSING)　　DR 污箱(DIRTY)　　DL 危标(DG LABEL)

左侧(LEFT SIDE)　　右侧(RIGHT SIDE)　　前部(FRONT)　　集装箱内部(CONTAINER INSIDE)

顶部(TOP)　　底部(FLOOR BASE)　　箱门(REAR)　　如有异状,请注明程度尺寸(REMARK)

除列明者外，集装箱及集装箱设备交换时完好无损，铅封完整无误。

THE CONTAINER/ASSOCIATED EQUIPMENT INTERCHANGED IN SOUND
CONDITION AND SEAL INTACT UNLESS OTHERWISE STATED

用箱人/运箱人签署　　　　　　　　　码头堆场值班员签署
(CONTAINER USER/HAULIER'S SIGNATURE)　　(TERMINAL/DEPOT CLERK'S SINGATURE)

Unit 4 Empty Container Release (发放空箱)

Exercises

Task 1: Listen to the following text and fill in each blank with one or two appropriate words.

Inland Haulage

Inland haulage is broadly ___①___ into two categories. That is Carrier's Haulage and Merchant Haulage. What is the difference between them?

Carrier Haulage means movement of the container from Point A to Point B under the control of the ___②___ using a haulage contractor nominated by the shipping line. In this case the consignee will pay for the same at the lines rate. This also means that when a line accepts a Carrier Haulage move, they should also ___③___ any claims or liabilities or damages that could arise during such a ___④___, unless it can be proved that it was caused by ___⑤___ of the cargo etc.

Such move would generally be ___⑥___ when there is a multi-modal transport involved-ex cargo moving from Antwerp to final destination Sandton (shown on Bill of Lading) via Durban/City Deep, where Antwerp is the Port of Load, Durban is the Port of Discharge and container is ___⑦___ from Durban to City Deep (rail terminal in Johannesburg) and further carried by ___⑧___ to Sandton door.

Merchant Haulage means movement of the container from Point A to Point B directly by the consignee using his ___⑨___ haulage contractor. In this case the consignee has the choice to ___⑩___ his own rates for the same. In this case, the line does not bear any ___⑪___ for the move and if there are any damages, they can hold the merchant liable for such damages. Comparing above ___⑫___ scenario, Merchant can arrange haulage either from Durban by road to Sandton door directly or take delivery of the container from City Deep and further move it to Sandton door by road.

Task 2: Fill in the blanks in the following sentences with the words or phrases given below. Change the form where necessary.

enhance	accommodate	depot	payload	inspector
pick-up	reveal	defect	exercise	standard

1. Container depots are an essential part of the logistics chain. At the depots importers can leave their empty containers and exporters can _____ empty containers for shipment.

2. For many shipping companies, the port of Rotterdam serves as the European empty

container collection point thanks to its numerous container _____ and high-quality service.

3. We are pleased to introduce you an "empty container pick up appointment" service. This new appointment service is created to _____ our service quality for empty container pick up to our valuable customers.

4. Each container in our fleet meets the Convention for Safe Containers (CSC) _____.

5. There are various types of containers _____ different needs: dry-van, open-top, high cube, open-side, bulk, flatrack, tank, refrigerated, and others.

6. To be a container _____ requires a basic knowledge of the construction and dimensions of containers.

7. It is important to make sure that the container can cater for the required _____ and possesses the necessary load-carrying capacity and the required volume.

8. Inspection of containers are made in order to _____ conditions that may be unsafe or which may reduce the usefulness or life of the container.

9. The types of _____ that may be found in containers are damage, wear, and non-conforming repair.

10. The user is expected to _____ reasonable care in operating the container.

Task 3: Translate the following terms.

1. container depot
2. pick-up container
3. drop-off container
4. inland haulage
5. merchant's haulage
6. 承运人拖车
7. 设备交接单
8. 空柜/吉柜
9. 重柜
10. 箱体检验

Task 4: Complete the following letters according to the Chinese words and expressions given in brackets.

Empty Container Inspection Advice

Dear All Customer,

Thank you for your support. It is always our o____①____ (目标) to improve our services to your good company. For improving the empty container r____②____ (发放), we would like to draw your attention on following highlight and appreciate you to coordinate with your a____③____ (约定的) truckers. Your c____④____ (配合) will definitely facilitate the container movement at POL and POD.

- It is our standard guideline to our appointed depots and terminals to release s____⑤____（完好的）and cargo-worthy empty container for loading export.

- Attached Container Inspection Advice is for effective reference to you and your trucker when p____⑥____（提取）an empty container.

- If any damages are found during pick up, please r____⑦____（拒收）the container and request a sound one.

- For special and heavy commodities, you are recommended to t____⑧____（拍照）for record before and during stuffing.

If any queries, please approach our local sales or customer service for immediate a____⑨____（协助）.

Thanks again for shipping with us and look forward to your continuous support.

Sincerely,

Emirates Shipping Agencies (China) Ltd.

Unit 5　Containers Stuffing
（装箱）

Containers Stuffing (装箱) Unit 5

Part A: Basic Knowledge Concerned

Text 1: Stuffing Plan*

Stuffing of a container refers to the process in which cargo is loaded into an empty container which is then sealed (often in the presence of customs), and transported to the carrier for loading on board a ship. It's also called vanning.

To avoid problems such as cargo overflow* or wastage of space, it is essential for shippers to have a stuffing plan before cargo is loaded into the container.

Measurement

Generally speaking, a 20′ container can hold as much as 28—30 CBM* or 980—1,060 cubic feet, while a 40′ can hold about 56—60 CBM or 1,980—2,110 cubic feet. The actual loading Internal Capacity of a container depends not only on the dimensions of the carton boxes* but also on many other factors such as the packaging material and the competence and experience of the stuffing personnel.

Weight

Besides the cargo's measurement, the weight should also be taken into consideration. It is important to note that in many countries the permissible weight limits for road and rail transportation are lower than the maximum payload a container can afford.

Use of Pallets

Palletisation is widely applied in some countries to increase cargo handling efficiency. When pallets are used, it is important to observe that:

- There are two major types of pallets, "Europallet" and standard pallets. The size of the "Europallets" is 800mm×1,200mm per piece while the size of standard pallets is 1,000mm×1,200mm per piece. A 20′ container can hold eleven "Europallets" in one tier or nine to ten standard pallets in one tier while a 40′ container can hold 23-24 "Europallets" in one tier or 20-21

---

stuffing plan
装箱计划

overflow
n. 溢出

CBM, cubic meter
立方米

carton box
纸箱

standard pallets in one tier.

- Wooden pallets* must be strong enough to allow storage of three tiers when loaded.
- Carton boxes must not overhang the edges of the pallets. On the other hand, boxes which utilize less than 90% of the pallet surface and do not align with the pallet edge can shift in transit.

In many cases, pallets are replaced by slip-sheets to save space. Some shippers use either pallets or slip-sheets in order to stuff more cargo into the container.

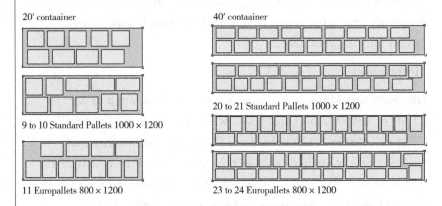

Text 2: Key Requirements of Safe Container Stuffing

It is of the utmost importance to recognize that actions taken when containers are stuffed may have direct implications for the stability* and safety of container ships, the lives of seafarers on board and the safety of others throughout the transport chain.

It is particularly important for all involved to understand the high degree of physical risk presented by the marine environment, the extreme forces to which a ship is exposed at sea, and the extent to which these risks are greatly increased by any failure to stuff containers correctly. This point cannot be over emphasized.

It is vital to adhere to* weight restrictions, and correct procedures for loading and securing* cargo, to ensure the safe distribution of weight and that cargoes inside containers do not move or shift when at sea, compromising the safety of the ship.

The IMO/ILO*/UNECE* Guidelines on the Packing of Cargo Transport Units provides a common global resource for information on container stuffing. Hence, the following requirements must be adhered to during container stuffing/unstuffing.

- Subject to booking request, select the most suitable container type to accommodate the cargo.

- Prepare a pre-stow plan before commencing stuffing so that weight/volume considerations are covered and point loading limits are observed.

- Never load by weight above the payload limits of the container, i.e. the cargo and container net weight must not exceed the container's gross safe working load.

- Never load by weight above the road regulations applicable on the transit.

- Distribute the weight of the cargo evenly over the floor of the container. Never stow heavy items in one section and light items in another. The weight of the cargo should not exceed the "60% within half the length rule".

- Do not stow heavy goods on top of light goods.

- Stow and secure all cargo tightly.

- Observe all the handling instructions on cargo such as "Do not drop" or "This side up".

- Stow goods with sharp corners separate from other softer merchandise. Use dividers and separating material as appropriate.

- Where possible with mixed loads, place packages containing liquid cargo on the bottom tiers with dry cargo on top.

- Use cargo liners for obnoxious* cargo such as hides* and carbon black.

- Do not use clamps or other loading devices unless the goods can withstand them.

- When loading Dangerous Goods, ensure that the IMDG Code packaging requirements are always observed.

- Do not load goods in a container with damaged packaging.

- Do not stow wet and damp goods with dry goods.

---

obnoxious
adj. 令人不愉快的，难闻的

hide
n. 兽皮

dunnage
n. 衬垫

- Do not use dunnage* or packaging which is incompatible with the cargo.
- Do not stow goods with tainting odours with sensitive merchandise.
- Observe all rules concerning dangerous cargo. Use appropriate labels and placards to identify packing and freight containers loaded with dangerous goods.
- Stow hazardous cargo near the door where possible.
- Include all necessary documentation.
- Record the seal number and the container number on all shipping documents.
- Never smoke, eat or drink during loading or unloading.

Part B: Business Letters

Sample 1: Customer Advisory — New Wooden Packing Material Regulation to/from Brazil

Dear Valued Customer,

Effective February 1st, 2016, the Port Authorities and MAPA* (Ministry of Agriculture, Livestock and Supply), will require the shippers to provide the Wooden Packing Material details for all cargoes to be loaded ex/to Brazil.

MAPA
农畜产品供应部

Therefore, with immediate effect, you are required to provide the Wooden Packing Material details for all cargoes to be loaded ex/to Brazil, by the time of Shipping Instruction submission to CMA CGM.

The Declaration must follow the below format:

- Wooden Packing: Processed Wood.
- Wooden Packing: Treated and Certified (the materials have been treated and/or fumigated and include a Certificate).
- Wooden Packing: Not Treated and not Certified (the materials have not been treated nor fumigated and do not include a Certificate).

- Wooden Packing: Not Applicable (when packing material is not wooden).

In case such information is not stated in the Shipping Instruction/Bill of Lading/Cargo Manifest*, we will be considering the option "Not Applicable" and the same will be declared at Brazilian Customs' System, being the shipper fully responsible by any penalty related to the non-compliance of such new regulation.

More details about this new regulation can be found on the following web sites:

www. agricultura. gov. br

pesquisa. in. gov. br

Thank you for your continued support. Should you have any questions or concerns regarding this change, please contact your local CMA CGM sales representative. For current schedule activity please visit our web site at *www. cma-cgm. com.*

Best regards,
CMA CGM (America) LLC

cargo manifest
货物舱单

Sample 2: MAPA Instruction

Dear Valued Customers,

Brazilian Agriculture's Ministry has published the *Normative Instruction No.* 32 in September, 2015. The instruction made the details of Wooden Packing Material as mandatory information for all cargo to and from Brazilian ports. The rule refers to packaging material made of wood and stuffed into containers.

With immediate effect, please indicate details of wooden packing material on shipping instruction by using one of the following three categories:

Wooden Package Processed: The packaging material is processed wood, a wood derivation made of fine wood carving plates.

Wooden Package Treated and Certified: The packaging material has been treated and/or fumigated, and with a certificate.

Wooden Package Non-Treated and Non-Certified: The packaging material has not been treated nor fumigated, and without a certificate.

If there's no remarks on your shipping instruction, we will declare "Not Applicable" to local Customs. Any circumstance, including but not limited to penalty, extra cost, or delay in cargo release, incurred due to incorrect or non-declaration shall be the responsibility of the cargo interest. Furthermore, the cargo interest shall also compensate for our damage or loss if we suffered because of your incorrect or non-declaration.

We would appreciate your attention to the above requirements and provision of necessary information to our local offices in timely manner. Should you have any question, please contact our local offices for further information.

Thank you for your continuous support to Yangming Marine Transport Corporation.

With best regards.

Yangming Marine Transport Corporation

Part C: Situational Dialogue

Scene 1: Talking About the Ways of Packing

扫码听音频

A: What are your conditions, Mr. Liu, as far as packing is concerned?

B: Well, as you know, we have definite ways of packing towels for sea shipment. As a rule, we use polythene wrapper for each article, all ready for shelf selling.

A: Good. A wrapping that appeals to the consumers will certainly help push sales. With keen competition from similar towel producers, the merchandise must not only be of nice quality, but also look good.

B: Right. We will see to it that the towels appeal to the eyes as well as to the purse.

A: What about the outer packing?

B: We will pack them six towels each with a different color in a box, ten boxes in a carton.

A: Can you use wooden cases instead?

B: Why wooden cases?

A: I am afraid the cardboard* boxes are not strong enough for sea transportation.

cardboard
n. 硬纸板

B: No need to worry about that. The cartons are lined with waterproof plastic sheets, and the cartons are made of cardboard; they shall be handed with care.

A: OK, but I am concerned that in case of damage or pilferage, the insurance company will refuse compensation* on the ground of improper packing, or packing unsuitable for sea voyage.

compensation
n. 赔偿

B: Well, if you insist anyway, we will use wooden cases, but the charge for than kind of packing will be considerably higher, and it also slows down delivery.

A: Then, I will cable home immediately for the final confirmation on the matter.

B: Please do. I will be waiting for your soonest reply.

A: I will call you up tomorrow. Good-bye, Mr. Liu.

B: Good-bye, Mr. White.

Scene 2: Talking About Container Stuffing

Carl Smith of ABC Shipping Company rings to Anna Hanson, who works at Brunner Trade Company, discussing the time of container stuffing.

Carl: Hi, Anna. Good day!

Anna: Hi, Carl. You too.

Carl: How about the container stuffing time?

Anna: Yes, I have checked with the factory. The cargo cannot be ready until at least 21:00 p.m. next Monday, so can I arrange container stuffing at midnight of next Monday?

Carl: Sorry, it's too late.

扫码听音频

ENS = Entry Summary Declaration
入境摘要报关单

cut-off
截止

Anna: Why? I have checked the CY closing time on the terminal website and it will be next Wednesday.

Carl: Right, but as I have mentioned before, the ENS* is cut off before 12:00 noon next Monday. Generally speaking, the CY closing time is cut off 48 hours before ETD, and ENS is cut off 96 hours before ETD.

Anna: I got it. But as you know, the vessel schedule is very important to us. We cannot delay the shipment at all.

Carl: Let me see. If you agree to pay the extra charge to keep the container out of the terminal and to wait until the cargo is ready, we can do the container stuffing at midnight of next Monday. Could you ensure the cargo quantity before ENS cut-off time?

Anna: Yes, we can.

Carl: Great. Before the cut-off time, the ENS information must be offered in time to ensure the cargo on board.

Anna: Okay, we agree. We cannot delay the schedule. How much is the extra charge?

Carl: It's 20′ GP. It's RMB 350/20′ GP.

Anna: No problem.

Carl: Thank you! Bye-bye.

Anna: Bye-bye.

Part D: Shipping Documents

Sample 1: Packing List

PACKING LIST

SHIPPER			
	Invoice No:	Page ___ of ___	
	Invoice Date:	Ship Date:	
		File Number:	
CONSIGNEE:		BILL TO:	

Containers Stuffing (装箱) Unit 5

(Continued)

SHIPMENT INFORMATION		
Customer PO No.:	Letter of Credit No.:	Mode of Transpotation:
PO Date:	Currency:	Transportation Terms:
Ref No.:	Payment Terms:	Number of Packages:
AWB/BL No.:	Incoterms Desc:	Gross Weight(kg):
QUANTITY	DESCRIPTION	UNIT

NO.	GROSS WEIGHT		NET WEIGHT	
PKGS	LBS	KGS	LBS	KGS

TOTAL:

Sample 2: Dangerous Goods Declaration Form

Dangerous Goods Declaration

Shipper/Consignor/Sender of Record	Transport document number		
	Page ____ of ____ pages	Shipper's reference	
	Booking No.	Freight Forwarder's reference	
Consignee	Carrier (to be completed by carrier)		
Vessel Name and voyage	Emergency contact telephone (with international access code)		
Place of receipt	Port/place of loading	Additional handing information:	
Port/place of discharge	Destination		
		Placards/Signs:	
Shipping marks	Number and kind of packages	Description of goods	Gross mass (kg)	Net Explosive Oty. (class 1 only)

(Continued)

Container identification number/vehicle registration number	Seal number(s)	Contatner/vehicle size & type	Tare mass(kg)	Total gross including tare(kg)
CONTAINER/VEHICLE PACKING CERTIFICATE It is declared that the packing of the goods into the container/vehicle identified above has been carried out in accordance with the applicable provisions. MUST BE COMPLETED AND SIGNED FOR ALL CONTAINER/VEHICLE LOADS (other than tanks) BY THE PERSON RESPONSIBLE FOR PACKING/LOADING		SHIPPER'S DECLARATION I hereby declare that the contents of this consignment are fully and accurately described above by the proper shipping name, and are classified, packaged, marked and labelled/placarded and are in all respects in proper condition for transport according to the applicable international and national governmental regulations. MUST BE COMPLETED AND SIGNED FOR ALL DANGEROUS GOODS CONSIGNMENTS BY THE PERSON RESPONSIBLE FOR OFFERING THE DANGEROUS GOODS FOR TRANSPORT PER IMDG CODE 5.4.1.1.11.		
Name of company packing container		Name of company of shipper		
Name/status of declarant		Name/status of declcarant		
Place container/vehicle packed Date packed:		Place and date		
Signature of declarant		Signature of declarant		

Exercises

Task 1: Listen to the following text and fill in each blank with one or two appropriate words.

Interchange of Container Load Goods

扫码听音频

The containerization is to integrate the break bulk cargo into an unit (container) which then is to transported by ship or other carriers. Except for the port which can serve as the spot of delivery and t ___①___ for containerization, the inland deport can also p ___②___ the role.

As for the FCL (full container load), the consignor will t ___③___ stuffing, counting, filling out the CLP (container load plan) and making seal. Usually, there are only two parties that take charge of the FCL, one is the consignor and the other c ___④___ . The carrier will undertake the duty of receipt and delivery of the unit which is under good condition and seal being i ___⑤___ . At present, the Container Liner operates the shipment of the FCL.

Containers Stuffing (装箱) Unit 5

As regard to the LCL (less than container load), the c ⑥ is responsible for the stuffing, counting, filling out the CLP and making seal at the CFS. The goods in the LCL involve several consignors and consignees. The carrier is in charge of taking and delivery of the goods in LCL which are in g ⑦ and seal being intact. Nowadays, the LCL Shipment Operator operates the shipment of LCL.

The spot of delivery is the place where the goods are delivered from the carrier to the receiver, the risk and expenses are divided based on the t ⑧ of shipping contract. At present, the goods in the container are delivered at the spots such as: ship's rail or hook/tackle, container yard (CY), CFS, and other places (door) appointed by parties concerned.

The v ⑨ of the delivery spots creates the variety of the delivery methods. As mentioned above, there are four places where the container load goods are delivered, which, therefore, can develop 16 varieties of d ⑩ (1. Door to door, 2. Door to CY, 3. Door to CFS, 4. Door to tackle, 5. CY to door, 6. CY to CY, 7. CY to CFS, 8. CY to tackle, 9. CFS to door, 10. CFS to CY, 11. CFS to CFS, 12. CFS to tackle, 13. Tackle to door, 14. Tackle to CY, 15. Tackle to CFS, 16. Tackle to tackle). In practice, in the seaborne container transport, the delivery methods CY/CY and CFS/CFS are more p ⑪ , the former is for the Container Liner and the latter for the LCL Shipment Operator.

Task 2: Fill in each blank with the most appropriate word given below in its right form.

evenly	crush	secure	improper	compliance
dunnage	liquid	bottom	dry	load

1. Packing a container tightly will help keep cargo _____ in place so it does not move around and become damaged.

2. Careful planning should be done before the time comes to _____ your cargo into a container.

3. Heavier items should never be loaded above items of lesser weight for risk of _____.

4. Containers of wet goods should not be loaded above _____ cargo.

5. If dry and wet cargo are loaded on the same level, _____ should be used to raise dry cargo off the ground to prevent damage in the event of leakage.

6. The weight of your cargo should be _____ spread over the entire area of the container's floor.

7. There are special laws and regulations that you are responsible for knowing and being in

_____ with for the shipping of hazardous materials.

8. Customs may examine your container if an X-ray shows _____ and unprofessional loading as it may be a sign of concealing unusual items.

9. Do not stack cargo all the way to the top in the back half of a container, but load over the entire area of the floor in the _____ half of the container.

10. Weight, size, density, and properties such as solid or _____, and even odors of commodities are factors to be considered when loading your cargo into a container.

Task 3: Translate the following terms.

1. stuff plan
2. packing list
3. payload
4. insufficient packing
5. container floor

6. 托盘
7. 木质包装
8. 集装箱容积
9. 衬垫
10. 纸箱

Task 4: Complete the following letters according to the Chinese words and expressions given in brackets.

Dear Mr. Xu,

Re: 1×40′HQ Booking to Spain-Container Stuffing

I am very sorry to a ___①___ (告知) you that your 40′ HQ container, which is doing stuffing at our warehouse, can't stow the whole lot. We were informed by our warehouse just now that there was around 4 CBM cargo l ___②___ (留下) at the warehouse as there was no more s ___③___ (位置). As I have mentioned to you before, 71 CBM exceeds the c ___④___ (容积) of 40′ HQ. Although we have tried and stuffed as much as we can, it is impossible to h ___⑤___ (容纳) all the cargo.

The left cargo is from your fifth factory: XXX. We shall appreciate it if you would check and advise us of your decision.

Yours sincerely,

Jason Bei

Unit 6　Laden Containers Gate-in
（接收重箱）

Laden Containers Gate-in
（接收重箱） Unit 6

Part A: Basic Knowledge Concerned

Text 1: Operational Procedures

Using its leading-edge* terminal management system and container handling facilities, YICT provides customers with efficient terminal operations. All procedures involving the movement of containers in and out of the terminal can be classified under three major sections: berth allocation*, yard planning* and gatehouse management*.

leading-edge
adj. 尖端的，前沿的

berth allocation
泊位分配

yard planning
堆场作业计划

gatehouse management
闸口管理

Container Pickup

- External empty tractors enter the terminal's parking lot at the gate and complete the application for container pickup.
- Drivers pick up containers at the designated location.
- External tractors exit via the exit gate after completing the required procedure; if sterilization is required, the tractors need to be sterilized* before leaving the gate.

sterilize
v. 消毒，杀菌

Gate Operation

- Handle container pickup and grounding application.
- Conduct inspection, weighing and sterilization of the containers.
- Container grounding.
- External tractors enter the parking lot at the gate after going through inspection.
- Drivers obtain container movement slips (CMS) indicating container grounding area.

- Drivers transport containers to the designated area as per the CMS.
- External tractors exit via the exit gate after completing the required procedures.

Container Yard Allocation

- The yard planning team arranges the allocation of containers in the yard.
- The terminal operation team deploys the equipment and tools required to handle the containers.
- For operations with special requirements, the terminal will make use of specialized equipment or tools.

Container Loading

- Shipping lines provide YICT with stowage plan* and loading list*.
- The yard planning team makes loading plans* as per the information provided by the shipping lines.
- The terminal operations team arranges for equipment and tractors to deliver the containers to the quayside and to load the containers onto the vessel as per the plan.

Berth Allocation

- Shipping lines or agents provide the terminal with advance notice of arrival times and of the quantities of containers for loading and unloading.
- The terminal operations team allocates cranes and berths as per the above information, notifies shipping lines and agents and on-site operators of berth allocation plans, and provides Customs, Frontier Inspection*, Pilotage* and other related parties with berth allocation plans.

Container Unloading

- Shipping lines provide YICT with the list of containers to be unloaded.
- The terminal operations team makes unloading plans as per the information provided by the shipping lines and arranges the yard area for stacking the containers.

---

stowage plan
配载图
loading list
装船清单
loading plan
装载计划

frontier inspection
边检
pilotage
n. 引航

- The terminal operations team arranges for equipment to discharge the containers and to load them onto tractors for delivery to the designated area in the yard for stacking.

Text 2: Difference Between Demurrage and Detention

Demurrage* and detention* are two words that often confuse people. Is there a difference between them?

- In the context of containerized cargo, in generic terms, demurrage relates to cargo (while the cargo is in the container), detention relates to equipment (while the container is empty after unpacking or before packing).

Let's see how it works.

Imports

A container is discharged off a ship on 2nd July. Consignee approaches the shipping line to take delivery of the cargo around 12th July.

Working off a standard 7 free days from date of discharge, the line free days (different to port free days) expires on 8th July.

So, the line will charge the consignee DEMURRAGE for 4 days from 9th to 12th July at the rate fixed by the line.

After the full container has been picked up by the client, for example, if they take another 7 days to return the empty container, then it is known as DETENTION which again will be charged at the rate fixed by the line.

So basically before the full container is picked up, demurrage is charged (after expiry of free days) and after the container has been picked up, till the time the empty is returned to the lines nominated depot, detention is charged.

Exports

In the case of exports, normally lines give about 5 free days within which the shipper has to pick up the empty, pack it and return it full to the port.

In case of delays more than 5 days, the line charges detention (generally same tariff as import detention) for the days that the empty is kept with the client as empty or full.

Once the container is packed and say for example the shipper is unable to ship the same due to any reason, then the demurrage will be charged at the rate fixed by the line till the full container is shipped out.

What I have mentioned above is the generic and most common form of use of these two terms.

There however is a difference in the usage of these terms by various shipping lines in various countries.

Some countries call it combined demurrage/detention, whereas in some countries it is shown separately.

In yet some other countries like Saudi Arabia and Japan, the term demurrage seems to be used to denote storage in the port/lines terminal.

Best option would be to check with the shipping line in your country how these terms are defined.

Part B: Business Letters

Sample 1: Late-come Application Letter

Dear Sirs,

Vessel/Voyage	HUOYUN V. 007E
S/O Number	GATU77897073
Number of Pkgs	143 CTNS
Total Measure	41.2 CBM
Gross Weight	15915 KGS

This is to inform you that the above-captioned cargoes will be delivered to your nominated* warehouse on or before 17:00 hour July 10, 2015.

nominated
adj. 指定的

We understand that at the time when our cargoes arrived at your warehouse, it is already out of the closing date and receiving hours of your warehouse.

To induce your operation, and in consideration thereof, we hereby undertake and agree as follows:

1. To pay you on demand all warehouse charges this may be, or appears to be, due and chargeable in respect of said shipment.

2. To pay the dead freight resulting from short delivery of subject cargoes.

3. To indemnify that all valid export license*, if any be delivered to your company on July 10, 2015 before 17:00.

export license
出口许可

4. To indemnify and hold you harmless from all demanded claims, liabilities actions and expenses including legal expenses and attorney's fees, which may grow out of or be connected with such operation.

Thank you for your kind assistance in this matter.

Yours faithfully,

CCC Shipping Lines

verified gross mass
经核实的集装箱总重

Sample 2: Implementation of the Verified Gross Mass* (VGM)

Dear Valued Customer,

According to the official notice of [Circular No. 92] from Ministry of Transport of People's Republic of China, effective from 1 July 2016, a packed container will no longer be allowed to be loaded on board vessels unless the shipper named in the Bill of Lading has provided its Verified Gross Mass (VGM) to the ocean carrier and/or the terminal representative.

"No VGM no load" policy will be strictly applied for all exports from China, at all terminals in China according to local MSA's guideline. We kindly remind all our customers to submit VGM via digital channels. Failure of submission VGM on time will result in container not loaded on decided vessel.

In addition, to facilitate the implementation of VGM, we have developed a page under *Maerskline.com* "World Factbook", where you will find vessels effective from 1 July and onward under cut-off deadline.

We thank you for your support for Maersk Line. We will keep you updated when any new information on VGM is available to share. For any questions, please feel free to contact your local customer service or sales representatives. You will find contact details of our local office at *www.maerskline.com*.

Yours sincerely,

Maersk Line Greater China Cluster

Sample 3: Customer Advisory — Vessel Delay*

vessel delay
船期延迟

Dear Valued Customers,

We regret to inform that STAR RIVER V. 0002S would delay arrival Laem Chabang from original schedule. It is reported the incident was affected by technical problem.

Here is tentative schedule:

Original Schedule: ETA LCH: 29—Jun—17.

Revised Schedule: ETA LCH: TBA.

We would apologize for this uncontrollable incident and updated situation is under checking and shall revert promptly.

Best regards,

Inbound Marketing

MOL (Thailand) Co., Ltd

Part C: Situational Dialogue

扫码听音频

Scene: Preparation for Loading

Duty officer: Is all the cargo ready for loading?

Foreman: Yes.

Duty officer: That's good. How many gangs* do you arrange for us?

Foreman: I try to arrange 4. But only 3 come now, the last one will come later.

Duty officer: Fine, when will you start to work?

Foreman: We can start at any time. They are standing by now.

Duty officer: When can you finish loading?

Foreman: If everything goes smoothly, we can finish in 2 days, to be exact.

Duty officer: I see, thank you. Do you have any plan for cargo loading?

Foreman: Yes, we'll first take in the general cargo, then the dangerous cargo, and the cases will be handled at last.

Duty officer: It sounds good. Please also tell your workers to handle the cargo with care.

Foreman: Ok, we will put a layer of plastic sheet over the lower hold before loading the cargo for later swift sweeping and collecting.

gang
n. 工班

Duty officer:	That's a good idea.
Foreman:	Do you have enough materials for lashing*, dunnaging*?
Duty officer:	We have enough materials on board. You can get them if you need.
Foreman:	Do we need to leave some reserved tonnage for draft* adjustment?
Duty officer:	Yes, we plan to have 150 tons. And you'd better appoint a watchman to check the drafts fore and aft.
Foreman:	Yes, we would cooperate to ensure the safety of the ship.
Duty officer:	Thank you in advance.

lashing
n. 绑扎
dunnaging
n. 衬垫

draft
n. 吃水

Part D: Shipping Documents

Sample: Dock Receipt

DOCK RECEIPT

EXPORTER (Principal or seller-name and address including ZIP Code)		DOCUMENT NUMBER	B/L OR AWB NUMBER
	Zip Code	EXPORT REFERENCES	
CONSIGNED TO		FORWARDING AGENT/FMCNO.	
		POINT (STATE) AND COUNTRY OF ORIGIN OR FIZ NUMBER	
NOTIFY PARTY (COMPLETE NAME AND ADDRESS)		DOMESTIC ROUTING/EXPORT INSTRUCTIONS	
PRE-CARRIAGE BY	PLACE OF RECEIPT BY PRE-CARRIER		
EXPORTING CARRIER	PORT OF LOADING/ EXPORT	LOADING PIER/TERMINAL	
FOREIGN PORT OF UNLOADING (Vessel/Air Only)	PLACE OF DELIVERY BY ON-CARRIER	TYPE OF MOVE	CONTAINERIZED (Vessel Only) ☐Yes ☐No

Laden Containers Gate-in **Unit 6**
（接收重箱）

(Continued)

MKS & NOS/ CONT NOS	NO. OF PKGS.	DESCRIPTION OF PACKAGES AND GOODS in Schedule B detail	GROSS WEIGHT	MEASUREMENT

DELIVERED BY：
LIGHTER _____
TRUCK _____
ARRIVED – DATE _____ TIME _____
UNLOADED – DATE _____ TIME _____
CHECKED BY _____
PLACED INSHOP ____ LOCATION ____
              ONDOCK
		RECEIVED THE ABOVE DESCRIBED GOODS OR PACKAGES SUBJECT TO ALL THE TERMS OF THE UNDERSIGNEDS REGULAR FORM OF DOCK RECEIPT AND BILL OF LADDING WHICH SHALL CONSTITUTE THE CONTRACT UNDER WHICH THE GOODS ARE RECEIVED, COPIES OF WHICH ARE AVAILABLE FROM THE CARRIER ON REQUEST AND MAY BE INSPECTED AT ANY OF ITS OFFICES.
		
		                FOR THE MASTER
		BY _____
		              RECEIVING CLERK
		DATE _____		

马士基中国航运有限公司　IN 进场

集装箱发放/设备交接单

EQUIPMENT INTERCHANGE RECEIPT

用箱人/运箱人（CONTAINER USER/HAULIER）		提箱地点（PLACE OF DELIVERY）	
		深圳盐田港	
来自地点（DELIVERED TO）		返回/收箱地点（PLACE OF RETURN）	
马士基中国航运有限公司		法国马赛港	
航名/航次 （VESSEL/VOYAGE NO.）	集装箱号 （CONTAINER NO.）	尺寸/类型 （SIZE/TYPE）	营运人 （CNTR. ORTR.）
马士基航运（中国—红海/ 地中海）/1104	MSKU5072313	外尺寸：6.1m×2.44m×2.59m 内容积：5.85m×2.23m× 2.15m/20GP	
提单号 （B/L NO.）	铅封号 （SEAL NO.）	免费期限 （FREE TIME PERIOD）	运载工具牌号 （TRUCK WAGON. BARG NO.）
3313	MSK3212	10 天	粤 A5737
出场目的/状态 （PPS OF GATE-OUT/STATUS）		进场目的/状态 （PPS OF GATE-IN/STAUS）	出场日期 （TIME-OUT）
出口装箱/完好		出口/完好	2011 年 3 月 6 日

(Continued)

用箱人/运箱人(CONTAINER USER/HAULIER)	提箱地点(PLACE OF DELIVERY)
出场检查记录(INSPECTION AT THE TIME OF INTERCHANGE)	
普通集装箱 (GP CONTAINER) ☐ 正常 ☐ 异常	冷藏集装箱 (RF CONTAINER) ☐ 正常 ☐ 异常 ||特种集装箱 (SPECIAL CONTANINER) ☐ 正常 ☐ 异常	发电机 (GEN SET) ☐ 正常 ☐ 异常

损坏记录及代号(DAMAGE & CODE)　　BR 破损(BROKEN)　　D 凹损(DENT)　　M 丢失(MISSING)　　DR 污箱(DIRTY)　　DL 危标(DG LABEL)

左侧(LEFT SIDE)　　右侧(RIGHT SIDE)　　前部(FRONT)　　集装箱内部(CONTAINER INSIDE)

顶部(TOP)　　底部(FLOOR BASE)　　箱门(REAR)　　如有异状,请注明程度尺寸(REMARK)

除列明者外，集装箱及集装箱设备交换时完好无损，铅封完整无误。
THE CONTAINER/ASSOCIATED EQUIPMENT INTERCHANGED IN SOUND CONITION
AND SEAL AINTACT UNLESS OTHERWISE STATED

用箱人/运箱人签署　　　　　　　　　　码头堆场值班员签署
(CONTAINER USER/HAULIERS SIGNATURE)　　(TERMINAL/DEPOT CLERKS SINGATURE)

Exercises

Task 1: Listen to the following text and fill in each blank with one or two appropriate words.

The terminal has strict driving rules and regulations. To ensure the ____①____ of everyone, you are requested to bear in mind the following rules while driving.

Entering/Leaving a Port Gate

- Please ____②____ when entering an entry gate.

- Please drive in the indicated lane when leaving an exit gate.

- For an empty container leaving an exit gate, the left door of the container shall be opened and ____③____ to avoid wounding people and damaging facilities.

- Maximum height and width limits in the ____④____ gate lanes: 5.0 and 3.0 metres respectively.

- Maximum height and width limits in the ____⑤____ gate lanes: 4.5 and 3.0 metres

Laden Containers Gate-in
（接收重箱） Unit 6

respectively.

- Maximum height and width limits for ⑥ in the exit gate lanes: 3.8 and 3.0 metres respectively.

- Maximum height limit in the side entrances and administration gate lanes: 3.8 metres.

- Over-sized cargo shall, subject to ⑦ of YICT Gatehouses, enter or leave the terminal via the specified lanes only. If necessary, ask the Control and Planning Centre to lead the truck.

- No ⑧ is allowed in the entry and exit gate lanes.

Parking Lot

- Park your truck properly in the ⑨ parking space.

- Do not park in ⑩ .

- Long-stay parking of a truck in the terminal is not allowed without the approval of the Duty Manager.

Truck Driving in the Container Yard

- Comply with the "Measures of YICT on External Truck Management".

- Maximum speed: 40 km/h.

- Slow down to look or stop to yield before crossing junctions. The speed limit when approaching or crossing junctions is 20 km/h.

- Give way to moving ⑪ . Follow the instructions of on-site ⑫ .

- Drive and park your truck according to ⑬ and line markings.

- Speed limit at the entry and exit gate lanes is 10 km/h.

Task 2: Fill in each blank with the most appropriate word given below in its right form.

overweight	stack	chassis	vessel planner	scale
shut-out	verify	reload	dock receipt	weigh

1. Most marine terminals in the US _____ export containers during the in-gate process.

2. All laden containers should be delivered to the nominated carrier's terminal before the CY closing deadline, otherwise you will be responsible for any charges arising from _____ due to late delivery.

3. _____ containers and mis-declared weights are becoming a very serious problem — it

is estimated that as many as 20% of containers are overweight or mis-declared.

4. As containers are _____ higher to keep up with the growth of world trade, overweight and mis-declared weights can lead to vessels being improperly stowed, which can adversely affect vessel stability and possible loss of containers overboard.

5. Overweight and mis-declared weights can cause damage to _____ and terminal handling equipment.

6. Dock Receipt (D/R) is a legal document _____ that a carrier has received a shipment at a dock.

7. Once the cargo is actually loaded in the container and the container is at an off-dock weight station, or during the in-gate process at a marine terminal, the accurate weight should be passed to the shipping line so appropriate action can be taken to load or move the container.

8. Each shipping line should have a process in place to ensure that the actual weight of the container is communicated to the _____ in order to arrange proper stowage on the vessel.

9. Shipping lines can arrange to have the overweight cargo _____ into a second container with all costs billed back to the customer.

10. A _____ is a document issued by carrier to acknowledge receipt of cargo at the carrier's shipping terminal.

Task 3: Translate the following terms.

1. Verified Gross Mass(VGM)
2. demurrage
3. detention
4. opening day
5. container grounding

6. 场站收据
7. 泊位策划
8. 设备交接单
9. 进闸通道
10. 集装箱堆场

Task 4: Supply the missing words in the blanks of the following letter. The first letters are given.

Customer Advisory for SOLAS Container Weight Verification Requirement

Dear Valued Customers,

The International Maritime Organization (IMO) has a ____①____ (采用) new regulations under the Safety of Life at Sea Convention (SOLAS) that require shippers to v ____②____ (核实) and provide the container's gross verified weight to the vessel master or his

Laden Containers Gate-in（接收重箱） Unit 6

representative and to the terminal operator for every p_____③_____（已包装的）container as a c_____④_____（条件）for vessel loading. These new requirements become effective on July 1, 2016. After this date, it would be in b_____⑤_____（违反）of SOLAS to load a packed container onto a vessel if the vessel master or his representative and the terminal operator do not have a verified weight.

KLine will continue to provide updates on this subject.

The brief summary for new requirement

The Verified Weight means the total gross m_____⑥_____（重量）of the loaded container as provided by the shipper (or a third party duly appointed by the shipper).

The shipper named on the carrier's BL is responsible to provide the verified weight.

The shipper may use one of two methods to obtain the verified weight：

Method 1—The packed container is w_____⑦_____（称重）after the end of the stuffing operation using calibrated and certified equipment.

Method 2—For some uniform or packaged cargo, the known weight of cargo packages/pallets/etc. and securing material is a_____⑧_____（加上）to the tare mass of the container.

Under either Method 1 or Method 2, the weighing equipment used must meet the accuracy s_____⑨_____（标准）of the country where the equipment is used. Also under either method, the d_____⑩_____（申报）of the verified weight must be signed and dated by the shipper or by its duly authorized representative.

Additional information

The World Shipping Council (WSC) and its member shipping companies have developed g_____⑪_____（指南）and FAQs (link below) to explain what the implementation of the regulations will require of shippers, vessel master or his representative and the terminal operator.

WSC Guideline：

http：//www.worldshipping.org/industry-issues/safety/cargo-weight

WSC FAQs：

http：//www.worldshipping.org/industry-issues/safety/faqs/

Sincerely,

KLine

Unit 7　Customs Clearance
（通关）

Customs Clearance (通关) Unit 7

Part A: Basic Knowledge Concerned

Text 1: Procedures of Declaration at the Customs

All customs procedures are divided into customs declaration, customs inspection, duty-payment, and customs release. All import goods, throughout the period from the time of arrival in the territory to the time of customs clearance; all export goods, throughout the period from the time of declaration to the time of departure from the territory; and all transit, transshipment and through goods, throughout the period from the time of arrival in the territory to the time of departure from the territory, are subject to customs control.

Customs Declaration*

Declaration of import goods is made to the customs office by the receiver within 14 days of the arrival of the means of transport; declaration of export goods is made by the sender after the goods arrive at the customs surveillance zone* and 24 hours prior to loading unless otherwise specially approved by the customs. Goods imported or exported at the customs office are declared in writing on paper or electronic declaration forms.

Inward goods confirmed by the customs to be mis-discharged or over-discharged may be returned to the place of consignment or imported upon completion of necessary formalities by the person in charge of the means of transport carrying the goods or the consignee or the consignor for the goods within three months of the discharging. When necessary, an extension of three months may be granted through customs approval. If the formalities are not completed within the time limit, the goods will be disposed of by the customs in accordance with the provisions laid down in the preceding paragraph.

Customs Inspection*

All import and export goods are subject to customs examination. While the examination is being carried out, the consignee for the import goods or the consignor for the export goods has to be present and be responsible for moving the goods and opening and

customs declaration
报关

customs surveillance zone
海关监管区

customs inspection
海关查验

— 103 —

restoring the package. The customs will be entitled to examine or re-examine the goods or take samples from them without the presence of consignee or the consignor whenever it considers this necessary.

Duty Payment

Customs duties are levied by the customs according to law.

The consignee of import goods, the consignor of export goods and the owner of inward and outward articles should be the obligatory customs duty payer.

The duty-paying value of an import item consists of its price, transportation fees and corresponding expenses, and insurance fees before unloading after the arrival at a point of entry into the territory of the People's Republic of China. The duty-paying value of an export item consists of its price, transportation fees and corresponding expenses, and insurance fees before loading after the arrival at a point of departure from the territory of the People's Republic of China. The customs duties are deducted from the duty-paying value.

Customs Release

Unless specially approved by the customs, import and export goods will be released upon customs endorsement only after the payment of duties or the provision of a guarantee.

Text 2: Customs Clearance for Imported Goods in China

There might be all sorts of issues to be dealt with by foreign businesses in customs clearance for their imported goods in China. Even though there is no success formula, attention to the following details should help ease the necessary clearance procedures.

1. The date of landing of the imported goods should be duly noted and the time and details of the shipment should be promptly checked to ensure that customs declaration will commence within the 14 day period prescribed by the customs. In the event of failure to make customs declaration within 14 days from the date of landing, the imported goods will be subject to a fine from the 15th day onward at a rate of 0.3% of the price of the goods calculated on a daily accumulative* basis.

2. Prior to the landing of the goods, all documents and invoices required for customs declaration should be prepared and checked

accumulative
adj. 累计的，累积的

before submission to the customs officer or agent for declaration purposes. A sum equivalent to the amount of customs duty chargeable on the imported goods should also be made available.

3. Throughout the process of customs clearance, a designated staff of the importer should keep in close contact with the customs officer or agent and promptly provide any documents required, such as product manual, copy of letter of credit, quarantine certification and trade agreements. Technical personnel should also be readily available to answer questions from the customs to facilitate the examination of documents and assessment of duty.

4. As soon as the customs duty demand note is issued, the customs duty and other relevant charges should be paid before the deadline so as to avoid paying overdue fine* (chargeable from the seventh day from the demand date).

> overdue fine
> 滞纳金，过期罚金

5. Should the customs require inspection of the goods, a technical staff designated by the importer should keep in close contact with the customs officer and answer on site or by phone any queries relating to the inspection.

6. Upon inspection and release by the customs, the imported goods should be promptly delivered or transferred in order to minimize warehousing or transfer charges. In taking delivery of the goods, the importer should inspect the external packaging of the goods. If the packaging is found to be damaged, the importer should suspend taking delivery and demand the warehouse operator or carrier to produce the valid commercial records.

Part B: Business Letters

Sample 1: EU Customs Update

Dear Valued Customer,

Having just passed the two-month mark since the beginning of the EU* Customs Advanced Manifest Rule, we would like to thank all our customers for your cooperation with us to ensure the smooth implementation of the rule. In addition, we would like to provide you with a number of updates regarding the rule:

> EU= European Union
> 欧盟

shipping instruction
装船指示

Deadline for Submission of Shipping Instructions* (SI)

We are pleased to inform you that Maersk Line is adjusting the deadline for submission of shipping instructions from 48 hours prior to CY cut-off to 40 hours prior to CY cut-off. Please note these new deadlines will automatically be reflected in your booking confirmations for your reference.

Submission of Shipping Instructions (SI)

We would like to encourage all customers to comply with deadlines for submission of shipping instructions (SI). Failure to submit the shipping instructions on time may delay submission of the cargo manifest, which could prevent your cargo from being loaded for export.

In addition, please make sure that your SI is filled out completely and accurately, in accordance with EU customs regulation requirements.

We recommend that you review the details below regarding information required by EU customs:

1. HS codes* (Harmonized System Code)

HS Code
海关编码，商品编码

EU regulations require you to provide either a HS4/HS6 code or a commodity description. We kindly ask you to provide us with the HS4/HS6 codes only, meaning codes of more than six characters long since codes that are more than six characters is not acceptable in EU Customs system.

2. Number of packages vs. piece count

EU regulations require you to specify the type and number of packages, not individual item counts. This means that customs may reject quantities such as "200,000" hats, as this represents the piece count and not the number of packages loaded. The correct format is "200 boxes containing hats" (i. e., the outer packaging). We urge you to provide us with the number of packages as explained above to avoid problems with customs.

3. Shipper/consignee's information

EU regulations require "complete" information about the parties involved (notify party must be available when consignee is "to order"). Although it is not very clear at this point what "complete" entails, we encourage you to provide us with as much information as possible (i. e., company name, complete address and telephone).

Cargo Data Declaration Fee (CDD) — Exception for Finland

The CDD as announced previously is (applicable to shipments gated in for export to/via the EU) applicable to all shipments with final discharge port in all relevant countries implementing EU customs rule and is set as USD 25 per Bill of Lading.

This charge covers:

- Day to day operating and administrative costs.
- Cost of interfacing with customs through 3rd party service providers.
- Fixed IT and admin costs of establishing interface either directly or through 3rd party to customs.

The CDD for cargo bound for Finland is EUR 25 per Bill of Lading and this exception is due to local charges by our feeder operator to Finland.

Thank you for your continuous support for Maersk Line and we look forward to future cooperation with you for your shipments to the European Union as well as to other destinations. We welcome you to contact your local sales or customer service representative for any questions. You will find contact details for our local offices on *maerskline.com.cn*.

Yours sincerely,

Maersk Line South China

Sample 2: Customer Advisory — All Export Cargo's Manifest to Chinese Customs

Dear Valued Customer,

We would remind you that as per Chinese customs rule, all export and transshipment cargo should be manifested and submitted to Chinese Customs and 100% in line with Shipping Instruction provide to Maersk Line. Any discrepancy among various export documentation will be regarded as incompliance* and the provider should undertake the risk or penalty by carrier and Chinese Customs.

incompliance
n. 不符

Here is the summary of all the export documentations which customers are obliged to provide and ensure the accuracy and coherence.

1. Pre-manifest submitted to the local vessel agency.
2. Export Customs Declaration sheet submitted to Chinese Customs.
3. Container Load Plan submitted to terminal.
4. Shiliandan of export cargo.
5. Shipping Instruction submitted to Carrier.
6. Any other docs which related to customs declaration.

We thank you for your always support for Maersk Line. For any questions, please feel free to contact your customer service.

Yours sincerely,

Maersk Line East China

Part C: Situational Dialogue

Scene 1: Lack of Documents for Declaration

Customs Officer:	Is this your declaration form?
Customs Specialist:	Yes. What's wrong?
Customs Officer:	There is no Commodities Inspection Certificate of non-wooden package for import goods in the attached documents.
Customs Specialist:	Commodities Inspection Certificate of non-wooden package? These goods are not from U.S. and Japan, so I think we needn't offer it.
Customs Officer:	According to the regulation, the goods imported from Korea should be declared with Commodities Inspection Certificate of non-wooden package since 16 February this year.
Customs Specialist:	Oh, it's a new regulation. I'll go to apply for it right away.

Scene 2: Talking About Customs Inspection

Maria Stacy from Five Star Shipping Agency is talking about the

inspection at the terminal with Jason Song, the manager of export department in Blackbird Furniture Company.

Maria: Hi, Jason. The broker has just informed me that your shipment has been selected by the Customs House for inspection.

Jason: Oh, tough luck.

Maria: The value of your cargo is high so it's easy to be noticed by the Customs House.

Jason: I see.

Maria: Could you check the shipping marks about this second commodity? And do you know whether it's stowed in the front of the container or in the second part?

Jason: Let me have a check. Please wait a moment.

Maria: Okay, it's in the second part near the door.

Jason: Great! It won't cost too much to open the container.

Maria: I will keep you updated with any updates.

Jason: Thank you, Maria.

After around half an hour, Maria gets the news from the terminal.

Maria: Hi, Jason, according to the updated information from the terminal, now the Customs House doubts if the name of the second commodity is on the sheet. Could you double check the material to make sure whether it's the same as it's shown on the sheet?

Jason: Yes, I am sure of it.

Maria: Okay, I will ask the broker to confirm the Customs House that the HS Code remains the same.

After several minutes, Maria receives the call about the result of the inspection and informs Jason.

Maria: Good news, Jason. Your cargo has been released by the Customs House at last.

Jason: Great! So can we catch the schedule vessel in time?

Maria: Yes, I think so. Time is enough.

Jason: Thank you very much!

Part D: Relevant Documents

Sample 1: Export License

中华人民共和国出口许可证

EXPORT LICENCE OF THE PEOPLE'S REPUBLIC OF CHINA

1. 领证单位名称 Exporter		3. 出口许可证号 Export License No.	
2. 发货单位名称 Consignor		4. 许可证有效截止日期 Export License expiry date	
5. 贸易方式 Terms of trade		8. 进口国（地区） Country/Region of purchase	
6. 合同号 Contract No.		9. 支付方式 Payment conditions	
7. 报关口岸 Place of clearance		10. 运输方式 Mode of transport	
11. 商品名称 Description of goods		商品编码 Code of goods	

12. 规格等级 Specification	13. 单位 Unit	14. 数量 Quantity	15. 单价（　） Unit price	16. 总值（　） Amount	17. 总值折美元 Amount in USD

18. 总计 Total	
19. 备注： Supplementary details	20. 发证机关签章 Issuing authority's stamp & signature 发证日期 License date

Sample 2: Customs Declaration Form

中华人民共和国海关出口货物报关单

预录入编号　　　　　　　　　　　　　　　　　　海关编号

收发货人	出口口岸		出口日期	申报日期
生产销售单位	运输方式		运输工具名称	提运单号
申报单位	监管方式		征免性质	备案号
贸易国(地区)	运抵国(地区)		指运港	境内货源地
许可证号	成交方式	运费	保费	杂费
合同协议号	件数	包装种类	毛重(千克)	净重(千克)
集装箱号	随附单证			
标记唛码及备注				

项号	商品编号	商品名称、规格型号	数量及单位	最终目的国(地区)	单价	总价审单币制	征免

特殊关系确认：	价格影响确认：	支付特权使用费确认：
录入员　　　录入单位	兹声明以上内容承担如实申报、依法纳税之法律责任	海关批注及签章
报关人员	申请单位(签章)	

Sample 3: Commercial Invoice

COMMERCIAL INVOICE

To: _____ Invoice No.: _____
                          Invoice Date: _____
                          S/C No.: _____
                          S/C Date: _____

From: _____   To: _____
Letter of Credit No.: _____   Date: _____

Marks and Numbers	Number and kind of package Description of goods	Quantity	Unit Price	Amount

SAY TOTAL: TOTAL:

Exercises

Task 1: Listen to the following text and fill in each blank with one or two appropriate words.

Commodity Inspection

Commodity inspection is a necessary ___①___ in executing an import and export contract. It plays an important role in import and export business.

Commodity inspection ___②___ the accordance of the quality, quantity, packing, etc. of the delivered goods with the requirements specified in the import and export contract. Also it testifies the ___③___ of the quality, quantity, packing, etc. of the delivered goods with the legal and administration regulations of the ___④___ country. In case of damage to the goods ___⑤___, the inspection certificates are necessary for the exporter or importer to claim compensation against the insurance company, shipping company, or other parties concerned.

Customs Clearance
（通关） Unit 7

Inspection ⑥ are documents issued by inspection institution. Upon inspection of the quality, quantity, or packing, etc. of the goods, certificates may be issued up to the requirements of the ⑦ . In I&E business, inspection certificates may be required for customs clearance, payment negotiation, or related claims.

The most commonly used inspection certificates are listed as follows:

- Inspection Certificate of Quality/ ⑧ /Quantity/Packing
- Veterinary Certificate
- ⑨ Certificate
- Disinfection Certificate
- Certificate of ⑩
- Generalized System of Preference Certificate of Origin (Form A)
- Inspection Certificate of ⑪
- Inspection Certificate on Damaged Cargo
- Inspection Certificate on Tank/Hold

The commodity inspection authorities shall conduct inspection according to the following standards.

- The inspection shall be performed according to the standards specified by laws and administrative regulations. These standards are ⑫ .
- In the ⑬ of the compulsory standards, the inspection shall be performed according to the standards agreed upon in transaction contracts. If the trade is conducted against the ⑭ , the inspection shall be performed according to the sample provided.
- In case the compulsory standards are ⑮ than the standards agreed upon in transaction contracts, the inspection shall be conducted according to transaction contracts.
- In the absence of compulsory standards, and inspection standards are either not agreed upon or agreed upon unclearly in the contract, the inspection shall be conducted according to the standards of the ⑯ country, relevant international standards or the standards ⑰ by the state inspection agency.

Task 2: Fill in each blank with the most appropriate word given below in its right form.

waiver	classify	revoke	lodge	infectious
cut-off	present	exempt	identical	data

1. The cargo-owner or agent is required to be _____ when the cargo to be cleared is examined by customs officer and also has the responsibility to move, open or restore the packing upon the customs' demand.

2. The relevant documents required for declaration can be _____ into three categories: banking and financial documents, commercial documents, and documents for government regulation.

3. For import clearance, the documents include import license, import cargo declaration form, Bill of Lading or airway bill, commercial invoice, declaration of non-wood package, packing list and documents on the basis of which tax reduction or _____ of inspection is claimed.

4. Please ensure to catch the planned vessel within the requested _____ time.

5. On arrival of a ship from abroad at the designated port, the Quarantine officers will go on board the ship to see if there are no _____ diseases being found on the ship.

6. Goods under duty reduction or _____ is a tariff preference measure that the state gives to the qualified enterprises and units.

7. There are two kinds of declaration form. One is electronic declaration form. The other is paper declaration form. Both are of _____ legal effect.

8. No matter in what form the declaration is lodged, either electronically or in paper form, the Customs deems the date when the declared _____ are accepted by the Customs as the date of the acceptance of declaration.

9. After being accepted by Customs, the declaration of import and export goods is not to be modified in any way, and none of the declaration documents can be _____.

10. How can I make amendments to the _____ import/export declarations?

Task 3: Translate the following terms.

1. Export License
2. Commodity inspection
3. Inspection declarer
4. Entry-exit
5. a letter of inspection attorney

6. 报关
7. 报关员
8. 装箱单
9. 商业发票
10. 保税货物

Task 4: Supply the missing words in the blanks of the following letter. The first letters are given.

Customs Pre-Clearance for Dangerous Goods into Saudi Arabia

Dear Valued Customer,

The Saudi Arabian Authorities have i ____①____ (颁布) a new requirement for consignees to obtain pre-clearance by the Saudi Arabian Customs in a ___②___ （提前） of at least three working days before vessel's arrival for dangerous goods with chemical properties.

Consignees are required to f___③___ （填写） in the attached form, submit it to the Saudi Arabian Customs for pre-clearance, and present it to the port authorities or local APL agent. Failure to obtain the pre-clearance before vessel's arrival or late notice in s___④___ （递交） the document will r___⑤___ （导致） cargo(es) being retained-onboard (ROB) the vessel.

The i___⑥___ （实行） date of this requirement will start on 12 December 2015. We would like to urge you to begin the customs clearance process for your dangerous goods/cargo(es) as early as possible with your consignee(s).

For assistance, please contact your local APL representative.

We thank you for your business and continued support.

Sincerely,
APL (China) Co., Ltd.

Unit 8 Cargo Handling at Container Port
(港口货物作业)

Cargo Handling at Container Port
（港口货物作业） Unit 8

Part A: Basic Knowledge Concerned

Text 1: How to Prepare a Container Ship for Loading Cargo

When a container ship is about to approach* a port for cargo loading, proper preparations should be made so that the cargo loading procedure can be carried out in a quick and safe manner.

| approach
| v. 靠近，接近

Container ships have special cell guides and lashing equipment in the under deck compartments* which helps in giving a secure stowage for sea transport. Efficient lashing and stowing of cargo containers on the deck is extremely important to prevent any kind of imbalance and loss of equilibrium* of the ship. Proper planning for cargo loading is therefore required and deck officers must know how to plan cargo container stowage.

compartment
n. 舱室

equilibrium
n. 均衡，平衡

This article explains the procedure for preparing a container ship and making it ready in all aspects to receive or discharge cargo at an upcoming port.

- All bilge alarms* should be properly checked for their working condition.

bilge alarm
舱底水报警装置

- All bilges should be emptied before the ship berths.

- An efficient ballast plan* should be prepared according to the pre-arrival condition of the ship. Proper consideration should be given to the fuel consumption while planning ballasting and de-ballasting procedures.

ballast plan
压载计划

- For securing containers, adequate lashing bars*, twist locks* and turnbuckles* must be made available.

lashing bar
绑扎杆
twist lock
扭锁
turnbuckle
n. 套筒螺母，螺丝扣

- Everyone involved with cargo loading and unloading procedure should know about different cargo handling equipment used on container ships.

- Deck crew in-charge of the cargo operation should make sure that all lasing bars are in position; so as to avoid damage to them or hatch covers* when containers would be loaded.

cover
舱口盖

- Turnbuckles and twist locks must be greased* and in proper

grease
v. 涂润滑油

— 119 —

	working condition.
defective *adj.* 有缺陷的，不完美的	• In case any defective* lashing equipment is found, it should be immediately replaced.
	• Proper lighting is must during cargo operation. Thus, ensure that the ship has adequate lighting facilities on deck, lashing bridge* and catwalks*. In case any lights are not working, they should be replaced before the ship arrives at the port.
lashing bridge 绑扎桥 catwalk *n.* 桥上人行道	• In case of loading of reefer containers, ensure that all reefer plugs are working properly and extra connections "Pig Tails" are available for maximum loading of refers.
spanner 扳手 actuator pole 开锁杆 stevedore *n.* 装卸工人	• Adequate spanners* and actuator poles* must be readily available for the stevedores*. • In case of any "Out of Gauge" cargo, extra lashing must be done. • Marking of the hatch covers must be clear and properly identifiable.
ventilator fan 通风扇	• All ventilator fans* in the cargo holds must be in proper working condition.
fire damper 防火挡板	• Ensure that fire dampers* for the cargo hold are in good working condition. • Timings and heights of low and high tides must be calculated prior to the loading/un-loading condition and properly displayed at the ship control center and the bridge.

Safety of the personnel should be of utmost priority while loading cargo. Deck crew involved with lashing and cargo activities must be extremely careful while working and should keep in mind the important points for safe container lashing.

Text 2: Container Stowage Planning and How It Works

What is Stowage planning—simply put—it is the act of allocating space to containers on board of a container ship in the order of the discharge ports.

Tools Required

• The scheduled list of ports that the ship will be calling at, in the order of rotation.

- A summary of the number of containers-size/type/weight of containers per port that are planned to be loaded on the ship.

- A summary of the number of hazardous, reefer and OOG containers per port that are planned to be loaded on the ship.

- List and summary of containers that are on board after discharge of the containers at your port. For the purposes of this article, we will consider this port to be Durban.

Definitions

Profile is the cross sectional view* of the entire ship covering both the deck and under-deck of the ship.

Bayplan* is the complete cross sectional view of the entire ship covering both the deck and under-deck of the ship, but displayed or printed per bay.

Bay* each container vessel is split into compartments which are termed as Bay and depending on the size of the ship it will proceed from 01 to 88 bays where Bay 01 is the bay towards the Bow* (the front) of the ship and Bay 88 is the Stern* (the back) of the ship.

Odd* numbered bays (1, 3, 5, etc.) means that it is a 20′ stow and Even* numbered bay (2, 4, 6, etc.) means that it is a 40′ stow.

Confused? Look at the below picture. I have used Bay 09/11 (10) and Bay 13/15 (14) as an example here. What you are seeing here is the cross section of the ship both on deck and under deck. Each of the small square blocks represents a 20′ unit space.

Row is the position where the container is placed across the width of the ship. If you refer to the above diagram, the Row numbers are circled in Green. It starts with 01 in the center and progresses outwards with odd numbers on the right (starboard) and even numbers on the left (port).

Tier* denotes at which level the container is placed-basically how high the container is stacked on board. In the above diagram, the Tier numbers are circled in Red.

---

cross sectional view
横剖面图

bayplan
n. 贝位图

bay
n. 贝位

bow
n. 船首

stern
n. 船尾

odd
adj. 奇数的

even
adj. 偶数的

tier
n. 层

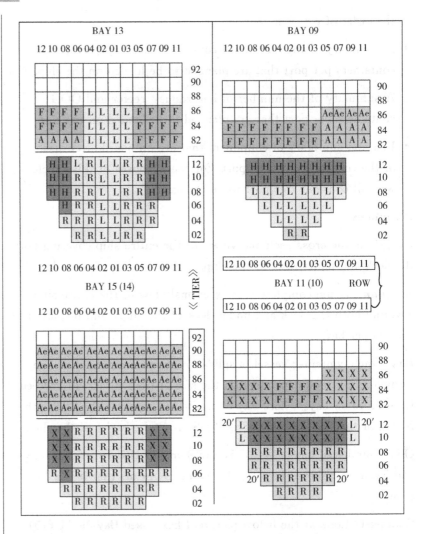

intermittent line
虚线

Hatch Covers (the dark intermittent lines* in the above picture) are the covers that separate the deck from the under-deck. The area above the line is called the deck (which is generally visible to us when we look at the ship) and the area below the line is called under-deck (which is not visible to us from outside the ship).

The planning is mainly done on a document called a "profile", which provides the full cross section of a ship at one glance. The enlarged version of this will be the actual bay itself. Currently, the stowage planning is mostly done via computers.

Although the computers do most of the work, the basis on which they work is the tried and tested methods that have been followed for many years around.

- The list of containers that are to be loaded on board are segregated by destination.
- Space is allocated to each of the containers. Firstly in the order of destination—the farthest destination at the bottom and the next port of call right on top. Secondly in the order of weight—the heaviest boxes at the bottom and lightest at the top.

For reasons of lashing and securing containers, a 40′ container can sit on top of two 20′s, but two 20′s cannot sit on top of 40′ (unless it is under deck and surrounded by other containers or within cell guides).

In the above profile I have used various alphabets and colors.

1. F for Felixstowe.
2. A for Antwerp.
3. Ae for Antwerp Empty.
4. H for Hamburg.
5. L for Le Havre.
6. R for Rotterdam.
7. X to indicate that it's a 40′ container.

The rotation for this vessel is Felixstowe, Antwerp, Le Havre, Hamburg and Rotterdam. So as you can see, Felixstowe containers are stacked right on top of other containers as this will be the first port of call after Durban.

Rotterdam will bethe last port of call hence it is right at the bottom of the heap... In this fashion the entire ship is filled with the containers that are to be loaded at each load port while also taking into account the containers that are ALREADY present on board from the previous ports.

If you notice in the image on the right, there is a container in stow position 110910 (Bay 11, Row 09, Tier 10)—circled in red and marked L for Le Havre.

Let's assume that this container was wrongly stowed for Le Havre instead of Felixstowe or a restow* was requested at a later stage to now discharge this container in Felixstowe.

restow
n. 倒箱

In order to reach this container, all the 12 containers meant for Antwerp (A and Ae) has to be "restowed" (taken off the ship and landed on the wharf side and put back on board once this box is taken out) because Antwerp is the next port after Felixstowe.

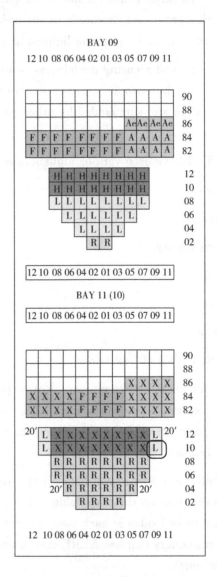

Then the hatch cover (the dark line between the deck and under deck) has to be opened to reach under deck.

Then the 1 container to Le Havre (L) in position 110912 must be "restowed" as well and only then the container in position 110910 can be discharged in Felixstowe.

As you can imagine, this involves considerable cost and wastage of

Cargo Handling at Container Port
(港口货物作业)

time for the ship to restow the $12\times40'$ containers and the $1\times20'$ containers to discharge this container that was stowed incorrectly.

So to avoid these costs and wastage of time, it is highly imperative that the right destination, right weight, and hazardous information if any is accurately passed onto the ship.

Each of the bays have deck stress or tier weight which is the maximum allowed weight that each of the tier/row can carry as per the design of the ship.

For example, if there are about 4 containers in a tier each weighing 26 tons, it may not be possible to accommodate all 4 in one tier as this might affect stability due to the heavy nature of the cargo.

However, if there are 5 tiers of empty containers as shown in Bay 15, it might be possible to load. These calculations will be performed by the computer itself and it will show up as errors.

Some of the most commonly used software for ships planning are CASP, MACS3 and Bulko. These use the BAPLIE file format structured by UNEDIFACT.

Part B: Business Letters

Sample 1: Suspension of Loading

Dear Sir,

We, as agents, wish to explain the suspension of ship's loading around 20:30 last night.

During her loading, one sling of fragile cargo suddenly fell down from the hatch way to hold bottom. The cargo was totally damaged. After the incident, both the ship side and the port side denied responsibility for it. The ship declared that such damage was caused directly by the winchman's* negligence during his operation, whereas the port said that the derrick* and steel wire were then not strong enough.

Now each party sticks to his own view and suspension of the loading was thus caused. The ship side already had asked the marine surveyor* on board for the inspection, the report of which will be

winchman
n. 绞车手

derrick
n. 吊杆

marine surveyor
验船师

later mailed to you. We will inform you immediately so long as the loading resumes. Please notes.

Regards,

YICT (China) Ltd.

Sample 2: Suspension of Discharge

Dear Sir,

Please be informed that above mentioned vessel has suspended her discharge due to two days heavy raining. She will resume discharging operation as soon as weather improves.

Regards,

YICT (China) Ltd.

Sample 3: Client Advisory — New Port Operation Announcement

Dear Valued Customer,

We are pleased to inform that Qatar Ports Management Company is confirming the opening of Hamad Port in Qatar effective from the 1st December 2016 replacing Doha with a better productivity and seamless delivery.

Hamad Port is fully equipped with modern technologies and equipment, which is located 40 km south of Doha, the capital of Qatar.

Port operator: Milaha & Mwani (Qatari Port Management Company).

Port code for the moment remains under QADOH; will keep all concerned appraised if there is any changes to it.

First CMA CGM feeder call will be the Al Bidda 628E, ETD Hamad 5th December 2016.

Tariffs of THCs, D&D and storage will remain unchanged.

Last container vessel to operate at Doha Port will be on 30th November 2016.

Cargo Handling at Container Port
（港口货物作业） Unit 8

Thank you for your ongoing support. Should you have any questions or concerns, please contact us at the concerned desk.

Assuring you the best of our services.

Best regards,

CMA CGM

Sample 4: Customer Advisory — Port Operation Updates

Dear Customers,

Subsequent to the earthquakes and tsunami* along the northeast coast of Japan on March 11, please find below the latest update of the port operations and our shipments. We will keep you posted of further updates once new information is available.

Port Operation

Operation of ports except Sendai, Hitachinaka and Kashima are resuming to normal. Please refer to *OOCL.com* for the latest updates of our vessel schedules.

Booking

Due to the significant impact on the normal port operation, bookings to/from Sendai, Hitachinaka and Kashima will be suspended with immediate effect until further notice.

Affected Shipments

All cargoes which are on their way to the affected areas, will be discharged at the Port of Tokyo or Yokohama until the three subject ports are back to normal operation or the port situation becomes more stable.

As Force Majeure* was declared for the vessel NYK Themis V. 13e09, cargo destined to Sendai on the subject vessel will be discharged at Tokyo, and it is customer's responsibility to make arrangements for cargo delivery at Tokyo. OOCL will contact affected customers individually for details.

Up to now, we are still evaluating the impact of the export cargoes from the affected areas. We will keep you informed of the latest updates of the situation. If you have any queries, please kindly contact our local customer service representative for more information.

---

tsunami
n. 海啸

Force Majeure
不可抗力

We would like to express our deepest sympathy and condolences to those who are suffering from this natural disaster.

Yours sincerely,

XYZ Company

Sample 5: Inquiry about Discharging Port

Dear Sir,

For the captioned container, the manifest reads Houston discharge and Charleston as place of delivery. As we can't find this container on stowage plan for Charleston discharge. Please advise by overnight reply if this container is to be discharged at Houston or Charleston.

Thanks and best regards,

ABC Company

Sample 6: Reply for the Above Inquiry

Dear Sir,

Thanks for your letter and sorry for our manifest mis-showing Charleston as place of delivery for subject shipment. Please stop moving it any farther and arrange discharge also delivery the same at Houston. Please correct our manifest accordingly. We apologize for confusion caused.

Thanks and best regards,

ABC Company

Part C: Situational Dialogue

扫码听音频

Scene: Shifting Some Containers for Some Reasons

Agent: Hi, Chief Officer, good evening.

C/O: Good evening, Agent. You look upset. Is there a problem?

Cargo Handling at Container Port
（港口货物作业）

Agent: Yes, something urgent.

C/O: Really? Just what is it?

Agent: Approximately half an hour ago, we got a fax from a very worried shipper requesting that 5×40′ containers under the B/L No. COSU2864129 be shifted right away from the lower hold of hatch No. 2 to the deck of the same hatch because your rotation for those containers has suddenly been changed.

C/O: My God, that's impossible! Our sailing time is 24:00 hrs midnight, and it's now already 7 o'clock p.m. We still have around 360 boxes for handling and lashing, so we don't have enough time to complete such an abrupt shift within the remaining 5 hours before departure. What's your opinion?

Agent: You are right, Chief, but the shipper of that lot of cargo said firmly that the containers have to be adjusted meet the sudden change of plan. For your information, that shipper has been our valued and stable customer for years. We sympathize with him and should give him the necessary help when needed.

C/O: It sounds reasonable. Nevertheless, the time left is really tight and what is more, our ship has to discuss the problem with chief tally and chief foreman first, so as to reach a common agreement in advance.

Agent: That's no problem, the shipper is now talking with them about the change. They will let you know later how it will go.

C/O: All right, I'll wait to hear from them. However, one thing I feel rather worried is that our sailing time will be delayed for another one or two hours. The container handling company will have to postpone our departure time somewhat, I suspect.

Agent: Oh, that's easy. I am going to talk with the chief foreman about it, and I will inform you of the result soon afterwards. Well, Chief, what you need to do now is to change you bay plan and get ready to shift those containers sooner.

C/O: All right, under such circumstance, on one hand, I'm awaiting your reply, on the other, I'm going to adjust my bay plan.

Agent: Very good, Chief, many thanks for your kind cooperation, I'll be back to you as quickly as I can, See you soon.

C/O: See you soon, Agent, thank you.

Part D: Related Documents

Sample: Laytime Statement Of Facts

装卸时间事实记录

LAYTIME STATEMENT OF FACTS

船名 M. S/S	ATLANTIC MERIDA （米乐达）	船舶登记总吨 Ship's G. R. T	33010.00		日期 Date	1st JAN, 2016	
装卸货物名称及吨数 Discharging		高粱（SORGHUMS）		Metric Tons of		49409.607	
船舶舱口数 There are		5		hatches on board this ship			
在本港装/卸货物舱口 Hatches Worked in the port No.		1、2、3、4		and	5	only.	
船舶装备装卸货通知发出时间 Notice of readiness tendered		时间 Time	1645	日期 Date	DEC. 29TH, 2015	星期 Week	TUE
船舶准备装卸货通知接受/收到时间 Notice of readiness Received		AS PER CHARTER PARTY				星期 Week	二
自 Work commenced		至 Work ceased		星期		记录	
日 Date	时 Hrs	时 Hrs.	Week	Week	Description		
29TH-DEC	—	1654		TUE	ARRIVED 13ZH GUISHAN P/STN AND NOR TENDERED		
	1654	1700			CIQ AND AGENT BOARDING FOR CARGO SAMPLING		
	1700	1830			SHIP FREE PRATIQUE & CARGO SAMPLING COMPLETED		
	1830	2230			WAITING FOR SUITABLE TIDE FOR BERTHING		
	2230	2400			INWARD PILOTS ON BOARD AND VESSEL PROCEEDED TO…		
30TH-DEC	0001	0442		WED	DITTO		

Cargo Handling at Container Port
（港口货物作业） Unit 8

(*Continued*)

船名 M. S/S		ATLANTIC MERIDA （米乐达）	船舶登记总吨 Ship's G. R. T		33010.00	日期 Date	1st JAN, 2016
	0442	0506		FIRST LINE ASHORED AND ALL LINES WERE FASTED AT BERTH NO. 2			
	0506	0600		INWARD JOINT INSPECTION CONDUCTED			
	0600	0800		INITIAL DRAFT SURVEY CONDUCTED AND COMPLETED			
	0800	0910		WAITING FOR CARGO DISCHG AS PORT RAINS			
	0910	1145		DISCHG COMMENCED AND CONTINUED			
	1145	1330		DISCHG SUSPENDED DUE TO STEVEDORES BREAK TIME			
	1330	1600		DISCHG RESUMED & CONTINUED			
	1600	1815		DISCHG SUSPENDED DUE TO PORT RAINS			
	1815	2250		DISCHG RESUMED & CONTINUED			
	2250	2400		DISCHG SUSPENDED DUE TO STEVEDORES BREAK TIME			
31ST—DEC	0001	0306	THU	DISCHG RESUMED & CONTINUED			
	0306	0800		DISCHG SUSPENDED DUE TO STEVEDORES/ GANGS SHIFTING			
	0800			DISCHG RESUMED & CONTINUED			
				DISCHG SUSPENDED DUE TO STEVEDORES BREAK TIME			
				DISCHG RESUMED & CONTINUED			
				DISCHG SUSPENDED DUE TO STEVEDORES BREAK TIME			
				DISCHG RESUMED & CONTINUED			
				DISCHG RESUMED AND COMPLETED			
				FINAL DRAFT SURVEY CONDUCTED AND COMPLETED			
				OUTWARD JOINT INSPECTION CONDUCTED AND GRANTED			
				WAIING FOR SAILING DUE TO PORT CHANNEL CLOSED BY GZ VTS EFFECTED			
				WAITING FOR OUTWARD PILOT			
				PILOT ON BOARD AND SHIP SAIL ING			

REMARKS:
1. PORT RAINS FROM 1800LT 29TH TO 0910LT 30TH DEC.
2. EXIT CHANNEL CLOSED BY VTS DUE TO MV CAPE VENUS ENTRY FOR BERTHING XINSHA PORT FROM 1200LT TO 1800LT 01ST JAN.
3. 01ST JAN—CHINA PUBLIC HOLIDAY OF NEW YEAR'S DAY.

_____ _____
As Master As Agent

Exercises

Task 1: Listen to the following text and fill in each blank with one or two appropriate words.

Cargo Work

The obligation of the carrier is to do everything necessary to deliver the cargo to the consignee in as good condition as when it was ___①___ to the carrier. The carrier therefore must ensure that all cargo handling operations, including the loading, stowing, carrying and discharging are done properly and ___②___.

Before loading commences at a port all ___③___ of a ship should be well swept out and ventilated to ensure that the space is clean, dry, odourless and without any ___④___ of a previous cargo. Besides, a stowage plan must be ___⑤___ carefully by the chief officer. He should also take into consideration the following principles in the handling of stowage and carriage of cargo.

The Most Efficient Use of space

This means that every cubic foot of ship's space must be utilized to the best advantage and the ___⑥___ reduced to the minimum.

The Highest Possible Port Speed

The distribution of cargo in the holds must be such as to assist correct and speedy cargo handling. It is customary to stow the cargo in ___⑦___ order of the intended discharge to avoid rearrangements of the consignments, and will not affect the ship's ___⑧___, trim or strength.

The safety of the Cargo

Pilferage of cargo parcels must be avoided by stowing them in such a way that they are ___⑨___ by heavier and stout packages. Valuable cargo must be stowed in a special compartment. Cargoes in the same hold or compartment must be ___⑩___.

The Safety of Ship and Crew

The most important thing is for the safety of the ship and crew. It means the total weight loaded must not exceed the ___⑪___ marks permitted. Furthermore, particular attention must be drawn to the proper manner in the use of equipment and labor provided by the port and also in the ___⑫___ of ship's gear to cargo handling procedures.

Cargo Handling at Container Port (港口货物作业) Unit 8

Task 2: Fill in each blank with the most appropriate word given below in its right form.

accessible	stowage	order	draft	load
reverse	TEU	handle	congestion	transfer

1. Containers are most often measured in _____ and are stowed in a cellular arrangement in rows, bays, and tiers.

2. The _____ of destinations should be considered when stowing the cargo onboard.

3. The cargo should be stowed in _____ order of the intended discharge to avoid arrangements of the consignments and adverse impact on the ship's stability, trim, or strength.

4. _____ plan is a completed diagram of a ship's cargo space showing what cargo has been loaded and its exact stowage location in each hold, tween deck, or other space in a ship, including deck space.

5. The stowage plan helps organize loading so that the cargo is _____ for unloading and quickly identifies the location and type of cargo for any given port.

6. Besides hinterland traffic, ports may compete for transshipment traffic, whereby larger vessels use a port to _____ cargo to smaller feeder vessels.

7. The load line represents the maximum _____, which shall not be submerged on her voyage.

8. After the cargo is stuffed into a container, it is handed to the container yard (CY) to be _____ on board according to the stowage plan.

9. Current domestic container terminal yard _____ equipments are mainly rubber-tyred gantry cranes (RTG) and Rail Mounted Gantry (RMG) crane two kinds.

10. Please be informed that below vessel delayed to depart from Shanghai due to bad weather, port _____.

Task 3: Translate the following terms.

1. stowage plan
2. bay plan
3. Bay/Row/Tier
4. container yard
5. lashing and securing

6. 装卸工人
7. 跨运车
8. 正面吊
9. 装卸
10. 前方堆场

Task 4: Complete the following letters according to the Chinese words and expressions given in brackets.

Dear Sir,

We have the p___①___(高兴) of informing you that we are agents for Union Fleet Co., Ltd., one of whose vessels, the M.S. Continent, has twice been to China with shipments of fertilizer for Shanghai, Tianjin and your port in August this year.

We have always r___②___(提供) our service to the entire satisfaction of both the Owners and Masters, and have bright prospects of acting as agents for other shipping companies. In the light of this encouragement, we are writing this letter to a___③___(使确信) you that we will render you the same untiring services as we are rendering to others in the event of our being a___④___(指定) as your agents for your vessels calling at Singapore.

We are well connected with the local business circles. Needless to say, this relationship is very u___⑤___(有用的) for canvassing cargoes under our agency.

For references about our company, you may i___⑥___(询问) of our bankers, the United Pacific Banking Corp. Ltd., Singapore and the Bank of China, Singapore.

Trusting that this letter will have your kind attention and looking forward to your favorable reply soon.

Yours faithfully,

The China Ocean Shipping CO.

Unit 9　Tally Work
　　　　(港口理货作业)

Part A: Basic Knowledge Concerned

Text 1: Container Tallying Procedure and Methods

Proper tallying procedure and methods ensure the effectiveness and efficiency as well as the correctness and accuracy of container tallying.

During tallying, a tallyman* will be assigned to each gang for the tallying of container ship, and more tallymen may join in if required in practice.

tallyman
n. 理货员

As far as the container ship for import is concerned, the tallyman effects his duty by the shipside or in the hold (for roll on/roll off ship). The tallyman must have a best knowledge about the requirements and notes in the Hand-over Record made by the Chief Tally*, and get an Import Bay Plan in hand, then check the series number of containers, and give the number to the slots in the same bay based on the discharging sequence and log off the Bay Plan, inspect the appearance and seal of containers, and in case any abnormal phenomenon is found, a record should be made to prove the fact.

Chief Tally
理货长

On the end of a shift*, the tallymen must check up the tallying figures with the consignee on the wharf or his agent and submit the finished container tally sheet together with the bay plan (with container being free) to the Chief Tally.

shift
n. 轮班

The process of tallying can be described as follows:

1. The tallyman effects his duty by the shipside facing one side of the container's door.

2. The tallyman checks the series number of the container discharged and inspects the appearance and seal and spots number on the Slots Plan based on the sequence of discharging, and if any wrong series number is found, note down the true number in the blank of the Slots Plan. During the process of discharging, in case any damaged container or seal missing is found, the tallyman must give notice to the terminal to stop operation, and report to the Chief Tally, who will ask the ship to look over. Moreover, seal-making will be done and the Damaged Container Record made up

for the ship to sign.

3. On the hand-over* of the shift, the containers undischarged in the bay plan should be spotted with signs, and notes of delivery should be made in details on the Shift Hand-over Record, and the date and signature of the last shift must be put down on the record. The tallymen of the next shift will proceed the work based on the work done by the last shift.

4. After the work a shift or after the discharging of one bay, the tallyman will hand over the container tally sheet and the bay plan (with container being free) to the Chief Tally for his inspection.

Text 2: Base of Tallying Containers

Bases for tallying containers are shipping documents which are selected and applied based on the mode of containers' movement.

Containers inward to or outward from a port in ocean shipping business must go through the indispensable procedure of tallying before discharging or loading, which involves several documents acting as the basis for the tallying of the imported or exported containers.

The basis for the tallying of imported containers is the paper called Import Cargo Manifest*. It shows the containers and the goods packed in the containers lot by lot carried on board in full particulars and their respective destination port.

In practice, the shipping company or its agent will provide with the information about the imported containers to the authorities of container terminal, ocean shipping tally and relative departments in stipulated time to ensure the container ship to the berth timely and get discharged smoothly. The documents concerning the imported containers involve the Import Cargo Manifest, Bay Plan and Dangerous Cargo List, etc. The Import Cargo Manifest, made up by the shipping company or its agent based on relative materials supplied after the completion of loading of containers (goods) aboard, lists the goods by lots about their Bill of Lading No., marks, packages, packing, description, weight, volume and their respective loading port, transshipment port, discharging port and destination, and also notes down the containers carried about their serial No., types, quantity, goods and delivery method as well.

As to the loading of container for export, the Export Tentative Stowage Plan is used as the basis for tallying, which also plays a role as an original proof to the containers that have been loaded on board the ship.

A shipping notice issued by the shipping company or its agent will be delivered to the container terminal company before the commence of loading. The Export Tentative Stowage Plan, complied by the Container Terminal Distribution Center based on the notice, is made up from the CLP which has been checked up with the customs' cleared D/R.

The Import Cargo Manifest consists of three parts, which is Stowage Plan, Bay Plan and Summary.

Text 3: Container-handling Technology

Proper selection of container-handling technology will not only save the expenses in the utilization of handling equipment and personnel but also raise the productive efficiency. There are two main schemes of technology applied in container handling.

Portainer-Straddle Carrier* Technology Scheme

straddle carrier
跨运车

In this scheme, the operation of "Ship-to-Stacking Yard" is carried out as such: the container is discharged from the ship by the portainer* (container gantry crane*) onto the ground of the quayside and then taken to the appointed slot in the marshalling yard* by the straddle carrier, during which, the operation of Yard-to-Yard, Yard-to-Container Truck, and Yard-to-Cargo Distribution Station, etc. is done by the straddle carrier.

portainer
n. 集装箱岸吊，码头货柜起重机
gantry crane
门式起重机
marshalling yard
集装箱前方堆场

The utilization of straddle carriers with its flexibility and multi-function can increase the handling rate of the portainer and shorten the period of operation, and implement by itself many tasks such as self-complaining, carrying, stacking and loading & unloading vehicles etc.

Portainer-Transfer Crane Technology Scheme

The use of the transfer crane* may be in the type of rubber-tired

transfer crane
搬运吊车，搬运起重机

RTG
轮胎式门式起重机，轮胎式场桥
RMG
轨道龙门起重机，轨道式场桥

horizontally
adv. 水平地
full-trailer
n. 全挂车

gantry crane (RTG*) or rail-mounted gantry crane (RMG*). At present, for the Chinese ports, the rubber-tired gantry crane is preferably applied.

As the gantry crane, for this scheme, cannot make interchange of the container directly with the portainer, the full-trailer is added in this scheme, that is, the container is carried horizontally* to and fro by the full-trailer* between quayside and stacking yard, between marshalling yard and rear stacking yard, and between stacking yard and cargo distribution center.

As the gantry crane is able to make higher stacking of the container, large amount of containers stowed can be obtained per unit area, and owing to a compact, stowing of containers can be made within the span of the gantry crane without waling space left, a higher utilization rate of the area can be made, both of which are of remarkable significance to a terminal with limited floor area of yard.

The adoption of the schemes of container-handling technology should take into account of the conditions of the terminal's facilities and the concerns of whether the scheme is practical and economical for the terminal.

Part B: Business Letters

Sample 1: Cargo Quantity in Dispute

Dear Sir,

Please be informed that M/V "Y" has completed loading at 15:30 hrs 12th. But the ship and tally company hold different opinions on cargo figures under B/L NO. 2. The tally report reads that the total quantity of 500,000 bags of cement was all loaded on board without any mistake. Nevertheless, the ship claimed a shortage of 480 bags on the basis of the crews tally.

The dispute between two parties is still going on. Under the circumstances, the relevant B/L is not to be signed. Perhaps her sailing schedule of 20:30 hrs this evening will be cancelled, should the problem be not solved by that time. Please note.

Best regards,

Sea God Line (China) Ltd.

Sample 2: Cargo Damage Settlement

A: Cargo Damage Claim

Dear Sir,

We have learned from the master of subject vessel that some cargo, while loading, was damaged by stevedores. In our opinion, we absolutely do not allow any damaged cargo loaded on board our ship.

Please contact the shippers concerned and ask them either to change it for some new cargo or to shut out the damaged cargo. We wish to have from you the final settlement of the case as soon as possible.

Thanks and regards,

ABC Company

B: Reply letter

Dear Sir,

Thanks for your letter, contents of which were conveyed to shippers immediately. They at last decided to offer new cargo as substitute after our loading discussion.

We are now very pleased to inform you that the said new cargo was already loaded on board. So the problem has come to an end.

Please note the above.

Regards,

XYZ Company

Part C: Situational Dialogue

Scene 1: Loading General Cargo Containers

Tallyman: Hello, Chief Officer.

扫码听音频

Chief Officer: Hello. What can I do for you?

Tallyman: We're going to load containers this afternoon. Could you show me the rotation of discharging ports on this voyage?

Chief Officer: All right. There are six discharging ports on this voyage. The first port is Hong Kong; the second is Singapore, and the next Malta, Hamburg, Rotterdam and Le Havre.

Tallyman: Have you got the pre-stowage plan already?

Chief Officer: I haven't got it yet. The planner hasn't come up till now. I heard from the agent that the containers may be over stowage this voyage. Some containers will be shut out. I'll give notice to you as soon as I get the pre-stowage plan.

Tallyman: Thank you. Do you need the whole stowage plan after loading completion?

Chief Officer: Yes, please piece up the bay plan of Dalian and Tianjin, and give it to me before the ship's departure.

Tallyman: OK. How many copies of paper stowage plan do you need?

Chief Officer: Two enough. Could you supply floppy disk to me? It will be convenient for us to discharge.

Tallyman: Certainly. Furthermore, we'll transmit the EDI information for the whole shipment to your company Dalian branch (or your agency) within one hour after your vessel's departure.

Chief Officer: What kinds of message could you supply with?

Tallyman: We have many kinds of message, such as the format of UN1.5, UN2.0, the NCD and the COSCO. It's up to your requirements.

Chief Officer: Both the format of UN1.5 and UN2.0 are available. By the way, could you supply us with the special containers list for the whole shipment?

Tallyman: No problem. We can supply you with the dangerous and reefer containers list.

Chief Officer: Thank you.

Tallyman: Not at all. Now, would you give me a copy of Xingang Bay plan? It'll help us to make out whole stowage plan.

Chief Officer: OK. Here you are.

Tallyman: Thank you. Bye-bye.

Chief Officer: Good-bye.

Scene 2: Talking About the Misloaded and Shifting Containers

扫码听音频

Tallyman: Chief Officer, are there any containers to restow?

Chief Officer: Yes, the vans of Dalian need to be loaded in the hold of Bay No. 49 and 51, so the containers on deck have to be shifted.

Tallyman: How many vans?

Chief Officer: Eight vans.

Tallyman: Where will you arrange them when they are rehandled back?

Chief Officer: It has not been decided for the time being. The planner hasn't come on board yet. I'd like to discuss with him about the particular stowage position for the shifting vans. I'll give you notice then.

Tallyman: All right. Do you want the new position to be shown on stowage plan?

Chief Officer: Of course. If so, it'll be very convenient for us to discharge them speedily at the discharging port.

Tallyman: Chief Officer, I haven't got the shifting containers' information in the particulars, could you give me a copy of the shifting list?

Chief Officer: OK, you may copy it now.

Tallyman: Furthermore, there is a container whose number is TGHU8306482, stowed at Bay No. 0390386 and discharging port for Dalian shown on our stowage plan, which was found at Bay No. 0390382 by our tallyman.

Chief Officer: Perhaps it was misloaded at previous port Osaka. Are there any containers to rehandle?

Tallyman: Yes, we have to shift two more containers above the Bay No. 0390382. Then we can handle the container TGHU8306482.

Chief Officer: Well, the total amount of shifting vans are increased to ten. It's your tallyman who found the misloaded containers in time. It's really excellent to your work!

Tallyman: Thank you.

Part D: Related Documents

CONTAINER DAMAGE REPORT
Without Prejudice

Report Number:

This document is to be taken as confirmation of damage having being noted to:

Vessel:................................... Voyage Number:........................

Container:................................ Shipping Line:.........................

REPORTED (Tick)
EXPORT
☐ On collection at container yard.
☐ On receival at loading depot.
☐ After loading.

IMPORT
☐ On collection at wharf.
☐ On receival at unloading depot.
☐ After un-loading.

APPARENTLY CAUSED (Tick)
☐ During loading.
☐ During un-loading.
☐ During transit.
☐ Unknown.

TYPE OF DAMAGE (Tick)
☐ Dent / Hole.
☐ Cut / tear.
☐ Pushed in / out.
☐ Water.
☐ Other................................

Comments:..
....
....

Name:................................ Signed:..............................

Date:................................ Department:.........................

All Business is undertaken subject to our standard terms and conditions of trading, available upon request.

Tally Work (港口理货作业) Unit 9

Exercises

Task 1: Listen to the following text and fill in each blank with one or two appropriate words.

Container Damage-checking Technology

In determination of the responsibility of the parties concerned for the container and the goods ___①___ any damage occurs to the both during the handling of containers, proper damage-checking technology means a lot for the tallying of containers.

1. For the container imported, the Chief Tally, before discharging, will consult with the ship about the dealing with the ___②___ damage of the container, the ___③___ of the damage record and the respective acknowledge and signing, and give specific requirement of the inspection to his tallymen and the ___④___. When discharging, the tallymen and the person sent by the terminal will make ___⑤___ and delivery by the shipside, and in case any damage is found or the seal broken or lost, the ship will be asked to be present to give a ___⑥___ and clear the responsibility, and the tallymen will ___⑦___ and number it on the record. In addition, the Chief Tally will make up the damage record which is to be signed by both the ship and the party being to ___⑧___.

2. For the container exported, the Chief Tally, before loading, will consult with the ship about the dealing with the damage of the container, make work records and give specific requirement of the ___⑨___ to his tallymen and the terminal operator.

When loading, tallymen and the persons sent by the terminal will make receipt and delivery. The tallymen inspect the containers ___⑩___, and in case any damage or the seal broken or lost is found, the tallymen will inform the persons sent by the terminal operator to look it over, and ___⑪___ the damage record and ask for signature. If the ___⑫___ damaged container or seal missing is found, an ___⑬___ notice must be sent to the ship for confirming; in this case, loading cannot be ___⑭___ without the permission of the ship.

3. For the ___⑮___ container(loading or unloading), if any damage or sealing undone is found, the tallymen will look it over together with the terminal, and a damage record will be made up for ___⑯___ and signing by the terminal and party concerned. And the responsibility of seal-making for the container with seal undone the terminal.

Task 2: Fill in each blank with the most appropriate word given below in its right form.

course	progress	count	divide	load
supply	legal	inspect	distinguish	stand

1. The tally report produced is recognized to have the effect of third-party notarization and certain _____ force.

2. Don't forget to cut off the electricity _____ before discharging the reefer container.

3. Tally Sheet for containers is an original _____ record made by tallyman for containers.

4. Daily report is a list for the chief tally to notify the _____ of the loading/unloading cargo to the ships.

5. Tally papers are the basis to _____ the responsibility of the shippers, ports, and shipping companies during delivery and taking delivery.

6. When accepting tally work, based itself on the _____ of the third-party and strictly observing relevant laws and regulations, as well as industrial provisions and standards, this company provides independent, objective, and unbiased tally results for customers and relevant parties.

7. Tally can be _____ into tally on shore and tally on board ships.

8. Tally sheet is issued by the tally company after its counting the quantity of the goods in the _____ of loading and discharging the cargoes.

9. You can make out a stowage plan according to the _____ list.

10. One works at the ship's side, examining the apparent condition and checking the container number and seal number. Another works on deck, _____ the container's top and jotting down its actual stowage.

Task 3: Translate the following terms.

1. tally sheet   6. 捣箱
2. loading list   7. 理货员
3. quay crane   8. 大副
4. import cargo manifest   9. 中转箱
5. type of damage   10. 工班

Tally Work
（港口理货作业） Unit 9

Task 4: Complete the following letters according to the Chinese words and expressions given in brackets.

Dear Chief Tallyman,

Here are some remarks for your attention:

1. The workers didn't discharge quantitatively according to the r ___①___ （要求）of the ship.

2. The cargoes ran short because the b ___②___ （破损的）package were not included at the original port.

3. The figures of the broken cartons were not included.

4. All the cargoes were tallied by my c ___③___ （船员）during loading and unloading. The quantity was clear and correct. We received and handed the cargoes according to the original data.

5. The ship will be f ___④___ （免除）from any responsibilities for the s ___⑤___ （短少）of the cargoes.

Best regards.

Master of M. V. SUNSHINE V. 007

Unit 10　B/L Issuance
　　　　　(签发提单)

Part A: Basic Knowledge Concerned

Text 1: What Precautions Should be Taken Before Signing the Bill of Lading?

A Bill of Lading is a receipt for the goods carried on ship, or technically put, is an evidence of contract between the shipper and the carrier. It is a documented title for the goods, signifying that the holder of the bill of lading is the legal owner of the goods it states. These days even on ships loading oil in bulk, the ship's masters are required to sign the Bill of Lading (B/L). Generally, there are separate departments looking after the cargo documentation and the authorization for cargo contracts.

However, the master* of the ship is still required to endorse the cargo carried on board for all legal proceedings. As a general rule, the master has the authority by law to sign the Bill of Lading on behalf of the ship owner*. Sometimes the legal jargon mentioned on the Bill of Lading can be unclear and confusing. It is therefore, essential that the master of the ship who is the owner's representative should thoroughly go through and if required be advised systematically before signing the Bill of Lading.

master
n. 船长

owner
船东

Following are the points that must be considered before signing the Bill of Lading.

The Shipper's Identity

The shipper is at a contract with the carrier which means that any information provided by the shipper if untrue could make the carrier liable. The shipper has to indemnify the carrier and may also have to back freight in this respect.

Therefore it is essential that the name, identity and addresses are clearly mentioned on the Bill of Lading.

Port and Date of Loading

The date of loading should coincide with the date as stated in the Mates' Receipt. This provides an indication of the origin of goods and is at times crucial to determine the customs duty structure or permissibility of the goods into a country.

Port of Discharge

Unless the charter party for a port to be nominated after the vessel sails to avoid deviation charges, the ship must precede with all dispatch to the port of discharge as said. The master must ensure that this falls within the charter party limits.

Condition of the Goods

Confirm that the goods have indeed actually or physically been shipped on board the ship. Check accordingly that an accurate description of the goods is present on the Bill of Lading, whether any short-loading* or dead-freights* are correctly mentioned. Ensure that all of the conditions must be in lieu with the Mates' Receipt and the bill may have a clause to reflect the actual condition of the goods.

Quantity and Description of Cargo Loaded

Prior to endorsing the Bill of Lading, the master should ensure that the quantity and description of the goods is true to its correct value of that loaded on board. This can be done by counter-checking the Mates' Receipt along with the other cargo documents.

Freight

Ensure that the Bill of Lading is not marked "Freight Paid" or "Freight Prepaid", as in certain cases, if not true. The master must confirm and verify the factual position of the freight with the ship owner or shipper.

It is also recommended to get a written confirmation from either of the two.

Conflicting Terms

No clause of the Bill of Lading should ever conflict with that of the charter party terms. If the bill has to be claused as per the charter party terms then such references must be clear and unambiguous.

Finally, check to see whether the number of original Bill of Ladings are in the set provided as stated.

Do you know any other important points that must be considered before signing the Bill of Lading?

---

short-loading
短装

dead-freight
亏舱费

Text 2: What does SHIPPER'S LOAD, COUNT & SEAL Mean?

SHIPPER'S LOAD, COUNT & SEAL or SLAC is a term that you would have seen in the description of the Bill of Lading for all shipments. What does it mean to the line and to the shipper?

In all break-bulk and bulk vessels, there is a document called Mate's Receipt*. This document is like a delivery note and has all the information pertaining to the shipment like cargo description/number of bundles/weight/measurement/etc. and this note is handed over to the ship at the time of loading.

mate's receipt
大副收据

This absolves the ship/owner/charterer of any claims relating to missing or damaged cargo etc. that might be levied upon them by the shipper at a later stage.

This was possible in the era of pre-containerization because the ship/agents were able to physically check and verify the cargo.

However, in the case of containerized cargoes and specially FCL cargoes, the carrier/agents are not privy* to the packing of the containers and the nature of the cargo. The carrier relies on the information provided by the shipper in terms of the cargo, number of packages, weight and measurement.

privy
adj. 私人的，不公开的

Hence the clauses "SHIPPERS LOAD COUNT AND SEAL" (SLACS) and "SAID TO CONTAIN" (STC) are put on the Bill of Lading to protect the carrier from any claims that the shipper might levy on them at a later stage.

For example, let's assume that the Bill of Lading states $1 \times 20'$ container STC 55 bundles of human hair and when the container reaches the destination and consignee unpacks the container to find that there is only 45 bundles. The Bill of Lading carries the above clauses.

As long as the seal has not been altered* or tampered* with, the consignee or shipper cannot question or hold the carrier liable for the shortage because the carrier was not present at the time of the packing of the container and carrier doesn't know what the shipper loaded, stowed or counted. Bill of Lading shows the details that was provided by the shipper, so the consignee must contact the

alter
v. 改变，更改
tamper
v. 篡改，损害

shipper to take up this issue.

If however, the seal number has been altered or tampered with, that becomes a totally different story for another day.

Part B: Business Letters

Sample 1: Letter of Indemnity for Telex Release

LETTER OF INDEMNITY

(TELEX RELEASE REQUEST)

Date	May/07/2016
To	HAPAG-LLOYD (CHINA) LIMITED
VSL/VOY	SUNSHINE V. 007E
S/O No	CCLU11038221358
B/L No & Date	CCLU11038221358, SEP/26/2016
Container No	TRIU8943343, CRXU1131335
Shipper	BB CORPORATION
Consignee/Receiver	CC COMPANY
Port of Loading	CHIWAN
Port of Discharge	SINGAPORE

We hereby surrender the full set of duly endorsed original Bill of Lading to Hapag-Lloyd. Please release the above shipment to the consignee without presentation of the original Bill of Lading.

We will pay to Hapag-Lloyd all incurred charges. We also agree that Hapag-Lloyd will be indemnified from all demands, claims, liabilities, actions and expenses, including legal expenses and attorney's fees, which may grow out of or be connected with such understanding or may result from any breach of this agreement herein contained.

Accepted by:

_____

Name of the Shipper

(Stamp and signature)

Sample 2: Guide to Endorsements of Original Bills of Lading

Dear Valued Customer,

The endorsement of an OBL is a legal transaction whereby the owner of the goods shipped transfers "title" to those goods by signing their name or rubber stamping on the back of the OBL. Proper endorsement is one of the requirements for cargo release. The party responsible for endorsing the OBL depends on who the OBL is actually consigned to. The notify party* on the OBL is not recognized in this instance.

notify party
通知人

OBL consigned to endorsement required by:

- To order of the shipper must be endorsed by that shipper.
- To order of bank must be endorsed by that specific bank.
- To order of the consignee must be endorsed by the consignee.
- To order must be endorsed by the shipper.
- Straight consignment to bank must be endorsed* by that specific bank.
- Straight consignment to other than a bank must be endorsed by that consignee.

endorse
v. 背书

Original Bills of Lading that are not properly endorsed as above will not be accepted for release of cargo. As an example, OBLs consigned as a straight consignment to "XYZ Import Company", endorsed by the shipper and/or the notify party but not the consignee, is not acceptable.

Please note that in the presence of a Letter of Endorsement from consignee, the OBL must be endorsed by the nominated party on the LOE to facilitate the release of the import cargo.

Should there be any additional information you require at this time, please do not hesitate to contact our team.

Best regards,

Loch M. Fraser

Logisitics Pty Ltd

Sample 3: Bill of Lading Requirement

Dear Valued Customer,

As a trade facilitator, APL endeavors to help our customers move their cargo across the globe seamlessly.

We would like to remind our customers with shipment inbound to Pakistan that a Master Bill of Lading is compulsory for customs clearance. The State Bank of Pakistan has further tightened its enforcement and will no longer accept Sea Waybill as a document for negotiation against import letter of credit or remittance against imports into the country.

As such, please ensure to submit the Master Bill of Lading for all your shipments inbound to Pakistan.

For more information, please approach your local APL representatives. We thank you for your business and continued support.

Sincerely,

APL

Part C: Situational Dialogue

扫码听音频

Scene 1: Talking About Main Functions of Bill of Lading

A: The Bill of Lading is one of the most important documents in sea transportation and is indispensable in world trade. What functions does it perform?

B: Well, the Bill of Lading is, in the first place, an acknowledgment by the carrier of the receipt of the goods entrusted to him for carriage by his ship to the destination as designated in the bill.

A: It signifies that the cargo shown therein has been received by the carrier for shipment or has been placed on board the ship, right?

B: Yes, and with this document the holder is in a position to take delivery of the goods at destination. In the second place, the Bill of Lading evidences the terms of the contract of affreightment*, on the basis of which the Bill of Lading is issued.

A: Can you explain it in details?

B: With pleasure, these terms include the name of ship abroad which the goods are to be carried, mode of payment of freight, ports of loading and discharge, responsibilities, liabilities, rights and immunities* attaching to the carrier and the law applicable, etc.

A: I see.

B: Finally, since the Bill of Lading is a document of title evidencing the holder's property in the goods, it is freely transferable and negotiable* and can be pledge for loans or as security or even sold and bought as commodities on overseas markets.

Scene 2: A Phone Call Conversation on Shipping E-Business

BOND: Hello, James Bond speaking.

JIN: Hello, Mr. Bond. This is Karen Jin from COSCO. I am calling to tell you that from now on, our e-business platform* can be used for your further business. You must have a try.

BOND: Eh, keep going.

JIN: Maybe you are not interested in it first. But I have to say, it is a new technology, and we would like to call it a time-saving technology.

BOND: How time-saving will it be?

JIN: Actually the new platform can help to minimize the time of inquiry, booking, and cargo tracking*.

BOND: I have to admit e-business or Internet have crashed my life already, for example, my wife now seldom went to the department store. Instead, she would like to go shopping online, it is more convenient and faster.

扫码听音频

B/L printing
提单打印

JIN: Indeed, our logistic network provides us with a lot of advantages. I believe you can taste the sweet if you do business with it. The platform has been tested by us. Lots of companies have tried it already and we've received quite good reviews.

BOND: Well, I'm wondering whether my staff can be accustomed to it quickly.

JIN: It is easier than you thought. If they have done the traditional business, it will be easy to get started.

BOND: Well, sounds great. What services does the platform offer?

JIN: The services we offer contain four main parts, which are Booking Assistant, Online Shipping Instructions (SI), B/L Checking and B/L printing* services.

BOND: I see, so what must I do first?

JIN: The first step is to log on our website and create an ID.

BOND: OK, I got it.

JIN: If you have further questions, don't hesitate to phone me. You got my phone number, right?

BOND: Sure.

JIN: Or you can also contact us via email or our website. There's an instant message page there. It's very convenient.

BOND: What an e-business age!

JIN: That's right. I think we are reaching a brand new era of cooperation. Very glad to talk to you, Mr. Bond.

BOND: Me too, I will call you if I can't cope with it. Good bye.

JIN: My pleasure, bye.

Part D: Related Documents

Sample: Bill of Lading

Shipper	BILL OF LADING	B/L No.
	BCD	
Consignee		
Notify Party	BCD OCEAN SHIPPING COMPANY	
*Precarriage by	*Place of Receipt	ORIGINAL
Ocean Vessel Voy. No.	Port of Loading	
Port of discharge	*Final destination	Freight payable at	Number original Bs/L
Marks and Numbers	Number and kind of packages; Description	Gross weight	Measurement m³

TOTAL PACKAGES (IN WORDS)

Freight and charges

Place and date of issue

Signed for the Carrier

Exercises

Task 1: Listen to the following text and fill in each blank with one or two appropriate words.

One of the most important documents in ____①____ trade is the Bill of Lading (abbreviated "B/L"). It is the basic document between ____②____ and carrier, and between shipper and consignee. The information it contains on the face of the printed form is as follows: name of shipper, name of consignee or his ____③____, party to be notified, name of vessel, ports of ____④____ and discharge, final destination(if on-carriage), place where ____⑤____ is payable and ____⑥____ of payment, ____⑦____ of cargo carried, number of B/L signed and date and place of issue. The terms and conditions are usually printed on the back of the Bill of Lading.

The Bill of Lading serves three distinct ____⑧____ in connection with the carriage of goods by sea:

- It is a receipt for the goods.
- It is ____⑨____ of the contract of carriage.
- It is a document of ____⑩____ for the goods shown on the B/L.

It is common practice to issue multiple original Bills of Lading, often three, for the same cargo. In each B/L there is such a stipulation as: "In witness whereof the carrier or his agents have signed the number of Bills of Lading, all of this tenor and date, one of which being ____⑪____, the others stand void." All of the originals are negotiable, but the cargo will be delivered to the person who ____⑫____ presents a valid B/L at the discharging port. This is not so that the shipper can sell the same cargo to more than one person; it is to ____⑬____ against any possible unreliability of mail service. Usually several originals will be sent to the same consignee by different means. In addition to the original B/L, a number of copies marked "____⑭____" on their faces are distributed to interested parties for their reference or use.

Task 2: Fill in each blank with the most appropriate word given below in its right form.

indemnify	surrender	exchange	title	cancel
cut-off	gross	negotiable	order	clean

1. Carriers cannot escape from claim of liability for cargo damage against _____ Bill of Lading.

2. A document of _____ means the freight can be transferred to the holder of the Bill of Lading.

3. There are two basic types of Bills of Lading, a straight Bill of Lading and an _____ Bill of Lading.

4. The BOL is issued by the carrier to the shipper in _____ for the receipt of the cargo.

5. A _____ BOL can be transferred by its consignee to a third party through signing (endorsement) and delivering it to another consignee.

6. One of the Bills of Lading must be _____ duly endorsed in exchange for the goods or delivery order.

7. We hereby undertake to hold you completely harmless and _____ against any claims which may be filed by the consignee.

8. You are kindly requested to authorize PENAVICO to correct the figure of _____ weight in the said B/L, enabling the shipper to get through bank negotiation.

9. If a carrier decides to agree to a request to switch bills then it is of paramount importance that all the originals from the set of Bills of Lading already in circulation be surrendered and _____ before the switch bills are released.

10. Shipping instructions must be received by carrier prior to the documentation _____ date/time for the applicable vessel.

Task 3: Translate the following terms.

1. House B/L
2. shipper
3. consignee
4. notify party
5. freight collect

6. 海运单
7. 倒签提单
8. 记名提单
9. 运费预付
10. 指示提单

Task 4: Complete the following letters according to the Chinese words and expressions given in brackets.

Angola-Release of Containers Without Original Bills of Lading

Dear Valued Customer,

Maersk Line would like to i_____① (通知) you that due to recurrent challenges to make overseas payments this year, the Angolan General Tax Administration (GTA) has issued a notice allowing Angolan Customs to hand over containers to importers without presentation of original Bills of Lading (B/L)/release from the carrier.

All parties on B/L must therefore be guided that the carrier has no c_____② (控制) over cargo once discharged. As a result, in case of cargo d_____③ (交付) to the Consignee by Angolan Customs without prior release from the carrier, the carrier will not be l_____④ (负责) for delivery of cargo without original B/L at the Angolan ports.

For any new shipments to Angolan ports, the following will apply and be included in our B/L:

"Merchants are expressly made aware that due to new Angolan Customs Regulations, Terminal o_____⑤ (经营人) are requested to allow delivery of import cargo without need of presentation of the Bills of Lading or release from the shipping a_____⑥ (代理). Discharge at Angolan ports is made at the merchant's r_____⑦ (风险) and the carrier's liability c_____⑧ (停止) after discharge of goods into customs custody."

As a consequence, Maersk Line strongly recommends that the shipper o_____⑨ (获得) payment for their cargo before loading at the port of origin.

Maersk Line is committed to support your business the best possible way under these circumstances that are beyond its control but will not be able to a_____⑩ (接受) any liability for cargo handed over to Consignees without our prior release.

Maersk Line will keep you posted with any further developments.

Yours sincerely,

Maersk (China) Shipping Co., Ltd.

Unit 11 Cargo Arrival and Delivery
（货物到港及交付）

Cargo Arrival and Delivery
（货物到港及交付） Unit 11

Part A: Basic Knowledge Concerned

Text 1: Import Cargo Release Guide

Send Arrival Notice*

Prior to vessel arrival, an Arrival Notice will be sent to the consignee or notify party via fax or e-mail for your convenience and as a courtesy.

Please note that the responsibility of cargo tracking remains with consignee.

arrival notice
到货通知

Issue Delivery Order*

Delivery order is issued to consignee or appointed trucker company (EMKL) against a fully and properly endorsed Maersk Line's Bill of Lading or copy of Seaway Bill*, along with consignee's letter of authorization* to an appointed person/trucker company for taking D/O.

Import Delivery Order will be available for release at the relevant branch office located in Jakarta, Surabaya, Semarang, Medan and Panjang.

delivery order
提货单

Seaway Bill
海运单

letter of authorization
委托书，授权书

Empty Container Return

The consignee (or consignee appointed trucker company) should bring the Delivery Order to return the empty equipment to our named Depot (as specified on the Delivery Order) within the equipment free time offered. If empty container returned above given free time then depot has the right to reject until payment of detention charges is settled.

Outstanding Charge Collection

All outstanding freight/charges, including but not limited to freight, demurrage/detention charges etc. must be paid prior to the issuance of Delivery Order or Cargo Release.

Diversions/Change of Destination (COD)

Should you need to change the destination of your cargo and you are the holder* of the original B/L, you must contact your local Maersk Line office to ask whether COD is possible and the cost incurred to perform COD. A written request must be submitted

holder
n. 持有人

using below form along with properly endorsed full set of B/L. If you require COD and shipper holds the original B/L, you must request shipper to approach his/her local Maersk Line office and submit the form there.

Text 2: What is a Telex Release*

You may have heard the term Telex Release several times in your day to day work especially in container shipping.

But what is a Telex Release?

In some instances, a shipper or exporter may surrender one or all of the original Bills of Lading that have been issued to them at the loading port.

Based on this surrender, they will instruct the load port agent to advise the discharge port agent that the cargo covered under the surrendered B/L may be released to the consignee shown on the B/L without presentation of any original B/L.

A Telex Release is simply a message conveying this instruction from the load port agent to the discharge port agent.

The shipper or exporter would request a Telex Release under below circumstances:

- The consignee at destination is a counterpart* office of the shipper. For example, if say DHL Global Forwarding is the shipper shown on the B/L and they are consigning some cargo to their office overseas, as there is no negotiation involved, they don't require an original B/L at destination.

- The shipper did not process his documentation in time and the ship that is carrying his cargo has already reached or reaching the destination and the original bills will not reach the consignee in time for them to clear before the expiry of free days.

- In some cases, an NVOCC operator might request for a Telex Release from the line so that they can issue their House B/L to their customer.

Technically a Telex Release can only be actioned when the B/L is issued as a Straight B/L* and not as a Negotiable/Order Bill or

---

telex release
电放

counterpart
n. 对应的人

Straight B/L
记名提单

Cargo Arrival and Delivery (货物到港及交付) Unit 11

Seaway Bill.

However, there are some lines that allow Telex Release on Negotiable/Order Bill of Lading based on surrender of the full set of Original Bills of Lading after verifying the endorsements on the Bill of Lading.

But why it is named Telex Release?

A telex machine is a teleprinter which can send and receive text based messages using the telegraph service. A message sent using the telex machine is known as a telex message.

A telex service could be used for real time one-on-one communication with someone on the other side of the world, or could be used to send a previously drafted message.

Telex was one of the most popular methods for communicating with ships while at sea and may be considered as the precursor to email communication.

The release instruction from the POL to POD is called a Telex Release because in the past, such release instructions to the discharge port used to be sent using a telex machine.

In its heydays*, a telex machine was used to transmit more than just cargo release instructions. Many people may remember having used a telex machine for the transmission of regular messages to the ships, preparing and sending reports before, during and after a ship's operation. For example, Arrival reports, Container Load Lists, Cargo Operations Progress Reports, and TDRs(Terminal Departure Reports)*.

heyday
n. 全盛期

TDR
离港报告

Although nowadays such OBL surrender information and release instructions are sent by email or updated in the shipping line's online system, the name telex release stuck due to the long period that the telex machine was used for such purposes and the quick communication that was possible using telex.

Text 3: Be Careful When Opening Container Doors

Amongst a container's weakest parts are its doors. The exposure to rain, condensation and a salty atmosphere causes the container door hinges* to corrode*. Such rust is not always visible, because

hinge
n. 铰链
corrode
n. 腐蚀,侵蚀

fatigue adj. 疲劳的 collide with 碰撞	repainting of the door hinge welds can conceal metal fatigue* corrosion. Containers also sustain damage during carriage or handling when they collide with* other containers or objects. Eventually, when workers open a defective container door, it comes off its hinges and can fall on anybody who is standing nearby.

Moreover, cargo and dunnage in the container can become unstable during the carriage or handling and end up exerting pressure against the container door. When the door is being opened, the cargo comes crushing down onto the worker. In one case, a huge paper reel, which had not been securely fastened, rolled out of the container and injured a stevedore fatally.

de-stuff 拆箱 personal protective equipment 个人防护用品 breathing apparatus 呼吸面具	Safety requires that containers are regularly inspected and maintained. Workers who de-stuff* containers must be properly trained on container handling and fully equipped with personal protective equipment* (PPE) such as a hard hat, high visibility jacket and safety boots. The workers should be aware of the nature and possible hazards of the goods. If the cargo includes chemicals, special equipment such as a breathing apparatus* might be necessary. A container door that is jammed or blocked should not be opened with brute force.
retaining strap 缚带	A retaining strap* on the outside of the container door prevents the container door from being forced open by cargo that presses against the inside of the door. The retaining strap is fastened around the door latches while the container door is still shut. After that the container door is opened and the retaining strap slowly released and eventually removed. Some workers have used equipments such as fork-lift trucks to brace the container doors, but such makeshift practices are not recommended without a full risk assessment.

Naturally, site instructions and safety procedures must be in place at the location of the container de-stuffing operations. The unloading area must be clearly marked. The surface of the location should be even (or descending slightly from the door end) without any slopes, debris or pot holes, in which case the container doors are less likely to fall open when released and any pressure on the doors from any contents inside will be reduced.

The container doors should only be opened right before de-stuffing commences. If machinery is used, everyone must keep a safe distance. A third party trucker who delivers the container to the unloading site should not be asked to help de-stuff the container, because he is unlikely to be properly trained, equipped or insured. If he has to be present at the unloading site, he is best placed and safest in his driver's cabin. The safety of every worker who opens and de-stuffs containers is markedly increased by established safety procedures and their rigorous enforcement.

Text 4: Opening Doors, When Things Are Not So Easy

On a particularly frosty morning when ice has seized a car door shut we would never consider using a crow bar. Conditions may be more extreme in container operations, but is it reasonable to use mechanical force to open or close container doors? Experience suggests that it is not—and often ends with someone being hurt.

Injuries to personnel involved with opening and closing container doors are increasing, and often it is as a result of an inappropriate technique that is being employed. We might expect container doors to open and close as if they were car doors, without understanding why this might not be the case.

Starting with the structure of container doors, most will have four or five hinges per door. The mechanics at the point of manufacture is that the hinge pins must be all aligned on the same plane (vertical and horizontal) and in line. Offset hinge pins will result in the blade binding when it is rotated about the pin—the more the misalignment*, the greater resistance* will be encountered during operation. At the time of manufacture, therefore, it might be expected that the hinge pins* on every door are aligned and free to fully open (270° of operation).

Let's assume that the container is presented in pristine* or well-maintained condition, why might the door not open with ease? Containers are generally either on a trailer/chassis* or on the ground, and in both cases the position of the locking gear handles are at an inconvenient height. For best results, the handles should be directly in front of you and at a height that is above the waist and below the shoulders.

misalignment
n. 不重合，未对准

resistance
n. 阻力

hinge pin
铰链销，折页轴

pristine
adj. 原始的

chassis
n. 底盘，车架

Technique is all-important. Start with the two lock rods on the right hand door, lift the handles out of the retainers and rotate them together as far as they will go. This should be more than 90° and rotation beyond 90° of ten initiates the door opening process by forcing the cams out of their keepers. Then grasp the vertical locking bars, one in each hand, so that your hands are just below shoulder height and pull back with your body, using your leg muscles rather than you back.

If the door is still stuck, unless specifically advised against doing so (for example, the container is carrying a flexitank or bulk cargo), open the locking bars on the left hand door and then grasp the inner locking rod of both doors and pull back, again using your body not your back. If the door still will not open, ask a colleague to pull on one door while you pull on the other.

Injuries almost always occur at the point frustration takes over and mechanical means are employed—the crow bar or a fork truck. So why will the door not open? Generally, this can be attributed to one of four reasons:

- The container frame is racked so that the door gear will not operate correctly. This may be caused by cargo shifting during transit. Look at the container to make sure that the doors are aligned and level, both top and bottom.

- The hinge pins and blade are seized due to corrosion.

- The door gasket* has been damaged and is preventing opening. Door gaskets are designed to present two or more fins against the structure or adjacent door. These are generally flexible but when the gasket is damaged, they may become hard or blocked thus jamming the door closed, or preventing it being closed.

- Water has become trapped between the doors and frozen, particularly relevant to refrigerated cargoes, or containers with moisture releasing cargoes in cold weather.

Doors that open but are stiff to operate may suffer from the first two reasons above, as well as misaligned hinge pins. Pins can become misaligned by damage to the "J-bar" which has twisted one or more pins or a repair to the hinge blade or pin that has incorrectly aligned the blade with the remainder of the hinges on the door. For example, adding a backing plate under a single hinge

door gasket
门胶边

blade will immediately take the blades out of alignment. Therefore, when a hinge blade needs to be refitted because of damage or corrosion and a doubler plate is required, plates should be inserted under all the blades on that door.

The safe operation of doors requires that some attention be given to them. Many hinges have coatings to the inner surface of the hinge blade, others use plastic liners, both of which are designed to protect against corrosion. Some designs are fitted with greasing apertures. Fundamental to success is the examination and maintenance processes.

Typically, doors will be opened for in-service inspections and off-hires*. Where oil does not free the hinges, repair work is necessary. These inspections include a visual check that the hinges and hinge pin welds are not broken or cracked. Opening doors could valuably be done when a depot releases a unit for packing, since it may have been in the stack* for a prolonged period.

off-hire
n. 停租，退租

in the stack
在堆栈

If the doors cannot be opened to pack a container, send the unit back! If it is already packed and you need to open the doors, but they will not open by hand, try to pull both doors open at the same time with increasing power. If you need more than two people, ensure you tell the container operator, especially if, as a result of opening the door, the locking gear or doors are or become damaged.

And, when you are opening a packed container, remember to watch out for those packages that are just about to fall out. In all these matters, be alert that the doors are big and heavy—treat them with respect and report anything unusual.

Part B: Business Letters

Sample 1: Letter From The Shipping Agent Informing of Arrival of Consignment

Dear Sir,

We have the pleasure to inform you that on board S. S. Jawahar, due at this port on 18th February, there are following goods for your account.

10 wooden case—Leather shoes

In order that we may effect customs clearance and despatch, we would feel obliged if you would let us have the Bill of Lading duly endorsed together with a letter addressed to customs & excise authorities, appointing us to act on your behalf.

Yours faithfully,

ABC Shipping Lines

Sample 2: Customer Advisory—Import Detention and Demurrage Calculation Change

Dear Valued Customer,

Please be informed that effective November 14th 2016 (based on container discharged from vessel at final destination) we will change the calculation method for our import detention and demurrage for customers with special extended free time.

Example:
  Special extended free time: 14 days
  Date of import discharge: 1 November
  Free time ends: 14 November
  Empty container returned: 15 November
  Detention and demurrage day: 1
  Previous calculation: USD 30 for 20 dry and USD 40 for 40 dry
  Future calculation: USD 50 for 20 dry and USD 70 for 40 dry,

Our tariff tier will remain the same as per below.

Container Type	Day 1-7	Day 8-12	Day 13-17	Day 18-Onwards
20' General Purpose Container	Free	USD 30	USD 50	USD 70
40' General Purpose & High Cube Container	Free	USD 40	USD 70	USD 90

Container Type	Day 1-5	Day 6-10	Day 11-Onwards
20' Reefers/Open Top/Flat Rack	Free	USD 50	USD 90
40' Reefers/Open Top/Flat Rack	Free	USD 70	USD 130

We thank you for your understanding and continued support. Should you have any queries, concerns or clarifications, please reach out to your local MCC Transport representatives.

Yours Sincerely,

MCC Transport Indonesia

Sample 3: Customer Advisory—China Customs Advance Manifest (CCAM) Rules Implemented in China Mainland

Dear Valued Customers,

Further to our previous Customer Advisories issued on China's 24 hour Advance Manifest Rules implemented in Shanghai, Xiamen and Nansha, we would like to update the latest announcement received on October 15th from General Administration of Customs* of the People's Republic of China who advised the advance manifest submission will be mandatory for all import cargoes that are discharged or transshipped at China mainland (except Hong Kong, Macao and Taiwan) with effect from 15th October 2014 (Beijing Time).

General Administration of Customs
海关总署

In order to meet this requirement, from 20th October 2014, CSCL will implement* a "No Document, No Load" policy for all shipments going into or transshipping via China mainland (except Hong Kong, Macao and Taiwan), which means all Bill of Lading information must be tendered to China Shipping's POL Agent no later than the deadline published by them.

implement
v. 实施，执行

To enable smooth transportation of your shipment after CCAM enforcement in China mainland, the following information is required in your shipping instructions.

- Exact place of delivery (UN/LOCODE code)
- The name and address for shipper and consignee (notify party is necessary when TO ORDER B/L)
- Container Number
- Payment method for ocean freight (Prepaid or Collect)
- Detailed Cargo description

- Number of packages
- Cargo gross weight
- Seal* number
- UN number and IMDG* code where applicable

If the full information can't be provided to customs before deadline, China Customs will issue DO NOT LOAD (DNL) instruction and it will cause the extra fees. CSCL will not load any shipment without getting loading permission from China Customs and such cargo will be rolled out to next available vessel subject to all associated charges and costs at shipper's expense.

More information about CCAM can be retrieved from following websites:

- Decree No. 172 in English:

  http://english.customs.gov.cn/publish/portal191/tab3972/module21538/info162113.htm

- Decree No. 172 in Chinese:

  http://www.customs.gov.cn/publish/portal0/tab3889/info105984.htm

- Notice No. 70 (2014) In Chinese only:

  http://www.customs.gov.cn/publish/portal0/tab49564/info720182.htm

Specific deadline for shipping instruction submission and first impacted vessel voyage will be communicated later. If you have any questions or require further assistance on the rules, please contact your local CSCL representative.

Sincerely,

China Shipping Container Lines Co., Ltd.

Sample 4: Letter of Indemnity* of Release Cargo Without Production of Bill of Lading

To China Shipping,

I am writing this letter of indemnity instructing you to release the cargo of 500 Orange Polo Shirts, to Mr. Paul Skelton of American

Shirts and Shorts, at New York port, without production of the Bill of Lading.

The document has yet to arrive due to admin errors, but I am confident that delivery to Mr. Skelton will not result in any concerns for any party involved. I have worked alongside ASS for several years.

I hereby agree to the following terms in consideration of you complying with this request:

—To indemnify you against any liability, loss or damage during the release of the goods to ASS.

—Should any legal proceedings be made against you in connection with this delivery, to provide you with adequate funds to defend?

—To deliver a copy of the Bill of Lading to you when it becomes available.

Yours Faithfully,

ABC Shipping Line

Part C: Situational Dialogue

Scene 1: Conversation Between Consignee and Carrier's Agent at POD*

A: Morning, Mr. Black. This is Smith, I am phoning to inform you that ship carrying your imports reached Tianjin port this morning and has started unloading in the afternoon.

B: Good news for us. Would you tell me when we can expect the goods to arrive at our warehouse?

A: Yes, there are three containers in all. We have to check all the orders of arrangement delivery today. The truck should arrive late Wednesday or early Thursday. When will you accept deliveries details?

B: I see. Could you deliver our goods by train?

A: Why? According to our arrangement we should deliver them by truck.

POD
卸货港，目的港

扫码听音频

B: We hope we can receive the goods as soon as possible. It's faster by train than by truck, isn't it?

A: Don't worry, we'll have no trouble meeting your delivery date. And if a customer requests a carrier other than truck, he must bear the additional charges.

B: Well, in that case, we don't insist on changing the mode of transport if you promise to deliver the goods on time.

A: All right. Thank you.

Scene 2: Agent at Loading Port Informs Agent at Discharging Port to Release the 5×40′ Containers

Conversation between Mr. Ma—discharging port agent, and Mr. Brown—loading port agent.

Brown: Hello, is that Shanghai Agency? This is Brown speaking New York Agency, USA.

Zhang: Yes, Mr. Brown, this is Zhang speaking from Shanghai Agency. May I help you, please?

Brown: I want to speak to Mr. Ma at your end. Is he in the office at this moment?

Zhang: Yes, he happens to be here, just a second, please.

Brown: All right, thank you.

Ma: Hello, Mr. Brown, this is Ma speaking, I'm glad to speak to you.

Brown: Me too, thank you, Mr. Ma. I am sorry to trouble you now. I need your help with the 5 containers we sent you. Do you know something about them?

Ma: Well, not yet. It's said that the consignee is still waiting for the original B/L from the shipper, therefore, the containers have not been released.

Brown: Right, that's what I want to talk to you about. In accordance with the written instruction from the shipper, the cargo cannot be released to the consignee even if the consignee has no original B/L in hand.

Ma: I see. But why was the original B/L not sent to the consignee in time, say 5 days ago? The container demurrage began to be paid from yesterday. If the original B/L had been given to the consignee earlier, the demurrage would not have happened.

Brown: Yes, nobody could have foreseen the problem. But because of the poor management between the shipper and the consignee, as well as the late solution of the Letter of Credit and some problem at the bank, the consignee has so far not received the original B/L. However, everything is settled now, so the shipper has agreed to release the cargo now to the consignee as quickly as possible.

Ma: Very good, In this case do you think you can E-mail us the written confirmation from the shipper, so that we may release the containers to the consignee accordingly?

Brown: Sure, I'll do it within ten minutes.

Ma: OK, I'll wait for it and meanwhile I am going to notify the consignee to come rapidly to my company to get the delivery order.

Brown: Thank you, I appreciate your good cooperation, Mr. Ma.

Ma: Oh, that's nothing, we should offer our good service to the customers.

Brown: You are right. Anything else, Mr. Ma? If there is nothing else, I would like to say good-bye to you.

Ma: Thanks, Mr. Brown, hope to see you again later.

Scene 3: Two Containers Got Damaged During Unloading

C/O: Hi, Agent, have you heard that 2 containers fell down and got damaged during unloading last night.

Agent: Yes, I have, but I have no idea about the details of the story. Could you tell me some more about it?

C/O: Certainly, here is the story. When I had just gone on duty and was busy with my work in the operation room, say 02:30 last night, I suddenly heard some faint but heavy sound from the direction of the deck. I soon sensed by instinct that some sort of accident had happened. So I rushed out of the room and hurried to the deck where I saw that 2

扫码听音频

containers had been seriously damaged. One foreman and two tallymen were also on the spot at that time.

Agent: Did any person tell you how it happened like this?

C/O: Yes, one tallyman who seemed to be the chief tally said that when one container had been lifted out of hold No. 3 and was in mid-air, it became difficult to be controlled because of it unusual weight. Therefore it hit another container below it, which fell down from the top of other containers to the deck. The container in the air got damaged and fell down onto the deck too, so both containers became seriously damaged.

Agent: I see. What about the cargo inside? Was it damaged?

C/O: I couldn't see the cargo inside, so I don't know exactly whether it was damaged, too.

Agent: OK, we'll check it later. What did you do then, chief?

C/O: I asked the chief tally to write me a damage report with his signature on it. I also asked the foreman on duty to sign it and then reported the matter to the captain.

Agent: Did you take any photos of the accident?

C/O: No, because it was too dark last night, but we took some clear pictures this morning.

Agent: That's good, Chief. What are you planning to do next?

C/O: Well, I am not clear how to deal with it best. I don't have much experience of this kind of problem. Can you give me some advice, please, agent?

Agent: In my opinion, you need to do the following things. Firstly, you should contact the port side via the chief tally to arrange for a cargo surveyor to come on board to inspect the damaged container. The surveyor will complete a survey report and you should get a copy of it. Then your ship should pass a copy of the survey report through your agent to the consignee, so that the consignee can make a contact with the port side in order to get some compensation from the insurance company. After the inspection by the surveyor, the damaged container can be discharged from your ship. Your captain should give a detailed report to your owner sometime today, either by fax or by E-mail, letting him know the true situation of the case. I think that's everything that should be done before you sail.

C/O: OK, that's a clear picture. I'll follow those steps, thank you very much.

Agent: Not at all. If you have any other problems, just call me and I'll give you a hand at any time.

C/O: Thanks a lot for your kind assistance.

Agent: All right, Chief, I am leaving now. See you again later.

C/O: Yes, see you again, Agent.

Part D: Shipping Documents

Sample 1: Delivery Order

DELIVERY ORDER

Transport Document No: Print Date:
Business Unit: Order Number:
Customs Ref. No: Release To:

Equipment Count: 5

Equipment No.	Size/Type	Tare Weight	Cargo Weight	Pin	Interim Pin	Properties	Condition	Quantity

Transport Plan

From	To	Mode	Vessel	Voy No.	ETD	ETA

Merchant Haulage Delivery Itinerary

Type	Name Release Date Time	Valid to Date Time	Est. Del. Date & Time	Reference
Full Delivery Pickup Terminal Empty Container Depot				

Haulage Instructions:

Sample 2: Arrival Notice

Communication from a carrier to the intended receiver that an international shipment is or will soon be available at its destination.

OOCL We take it personally	ARRIVAL NOTICE Revised	BILL OF LADING NO. OOLU3061276960 SHIPPER REFERENCE: PO NUMBER:
SHIPPER	CONSIGNEE	NOTIFY PARTY
IB HAULAGE DOOR DELIVERY	BROKER	Customs Clear Loc#:2709 Customs Clear City: Long Beach IT Date: SCAC Code: OOLU
Vessel/Voyage arriving at POD OOCL NINGBO 074	ESTIMATE ARRIVAL POD at: Long Beach on EST CARGO AVAILABLE at: Long Beach on Friday, March 23, 2012 3:00 PM	
Place of Receipt Hong Kong, Hong Kong	Port of Loading Hong Kong	Cargo Pickup Location: LGB01 Long Beach Container Terminal 1171 Pier F Avenue, Berth F-10 United States 1-562-435-8585 FIRMS W183
Port of Discharge Long Beach	Place of Delivery Long Beach, Los Angeles, California, United States	

OOCL We take it personally	ARRIVAL NOTICE Revised	BILL OF LADING NO. OOLU3061276350 SHIPPER REFERENCE: PO NUMBER:
SHIPPER	CONSIGNEE	NOTIFY PARTY
IB HAULAGE MERCHANT CY	BROKER	Customs Clear Loc#: 3901 Customs Clear City: Chicago IT Date: 23 Jan 2012
Vessel/Voyage arriving at POD CHICAGO BRIDGE 053 E	ESTIMATE ARRIVAL POD at: Long Beach on Monday, January 23, 2012 8:00 AM EST CARGO AVAILABLE at: Long Beach on Friday, January 27, 2012 4:00 PM	
Place of Receipt Hong Kong, Hong Kong	Port of Loading Hong Kong	Cargo Pickup Location: JOL20 BNSF-Chicago/Joliet(LPC) Chicago Ramp 26664 South Baseline Road, Elwood, IL 60421, USA. FIRMS H572
Port of Discharge Long Beach	Place of Delivery Long Beach, Los Angeles, California, United States	

Cargo Arrival and Delivery (货物到港及交付) Unit 11

Exercises

Task 1: Listen to the following text and fill in each blank with one or two appropriate words.

Unloading a Container Ship

The ship has a detailed cargo plan. The plan has the ___①___ of each container on the ship and the port for its delivery. The containers that need to be taken off at the port are ___②___ in groups.

The plan is needed so the ___③___ operator knows which containers to take off the ship. The planners make sure that the crane operator does not need to move too many containers around to get to the ones they need to unload.

Once the required containers are unloaded, the ship may still have many containers to be delivered to other ports. The ship will have a new ___④___ that shows the crane operator where to stack new containers.

As part of the cargo plan, the ___⑤___ of the containers is spread ___⑥___ over the ship. This prevents the ship from becoming ___⑦___.

Using the cargo plan, the ___⑧___ select the containers to unload from the ship. Stevedores operate the cranes and ___⑨___ the loaded containers. A ___⑩___ hangs from the crane. There are four smaller lifting cables that hang from the spreader. Fittings on each corner of the container are ___⑪___ onto the four smaller cables by the stevedores.

Waiting on the wharf below the crane will be a ___⑫___ or forklift. Once in place, the lifting cables will be unlocked from the spreader or the container itself.

The container is driven to a ___⑬___ where it will be stacked with others that will be transported to the same location.

Because of the weight of loaded containers they should only be handled with spreaders which are the same size as the top of the container. Empty containers can be lifted by the four lifting wires or by a simple forklift lifting it from the ___⑭___ of the container's base.

While the ship is being unloaded, the ___⑮___ may need to pump water into ___⑯___ to keep the ship balanced.

Task 2: Fill in each blank with the most appropriate word given below in its right form.

rely on	transfer	release	berth	congestion
go through	attention	schedule	failure	acknowledge

1. Delivery order is an order from a shipping line to the terminal superintendent for the _____ of goods to a consignee following payment of freight charges.

2. Delivery order is the necessary document to _____ the importing country's customs formalities and the evidence of taking delivery of goods.

3. Import containers are not weighed prior to out-gate from marine terminals, and shipping lines _____ the Bill of Lading weight supplied by the shipper overseas to determine what action needs to be taken to safely and legally move the container.

4. For overweight inbound containers, shipping lines can switch the Bill of Lading to "port to port" and force the consignee or shipper to arrange for trucking at their expense, and _____ risk for any fines or penalties that may result.

5. Ports around the U.S. are experiencing _____ due to the traditional increase in imports for the holiday shopping season.

6. For good preparations before your ship's arrival at our port, we need your advice of the ship's _____ 7 days in advance, enabling us to attend to the entry formalities in time.

7. We had to _____ our ship without the aid of tugboats.

8. When the merchandise was received, the consignee executed the delivery receipt and _____ that the freight was received in good condition, except as noted.

9. When your freight is lost or damaged upon arrival, it is important to give _____ to the issue immediately.

10. Since you are responsible for the _____ to accept the freight, you could be on the hook for storage and processing fees.

Task 3: Translate the following terms.

1. Mini Land-bridge(MLB)
2. Delivery Order
3. Arrival Notice
4. Telex Release
5. Proof of Delivery
6. 进口许可
7. 进口舱单
8. 进口清关
9. 保函
10. 拆箱

Task 4: Supply the missing words in the blanks of the following letter. The first letters are given.

Arrival Delays Due to South California Port Congestion

Dear Valued Customer,

Please be alerted that c_____ ① (拥挤) at the ports of Los Angeles and Long Beach has reached a critical point. Several container ships are anchoring off the harbor and waiting in line to b_____② _____(靠泊). Vessels alongside are either not undergoing cargo work or delayed in working due to a s_____③_____(缺少) of ILWU (International Longshore and Warehouse Union) labor.

Consequently, later-than-scheduled arrivals for the following services can be expected at the ports of Los Angeles and Long Beach, and beyond:

- ACA (Asia Central America Service)
- CC1 (Central China 1)
- CC2 (Central China 2)
- CC3 (Central China 3)
- CC4 (Central China 4)
- PA1 (Panama Atlantic 1)
- PA2 (Panama Atlantic 2)
- SC1 (South China 1)
- SC2 (South China 2)
- SE1 (Southeast Asia 1)
- SE2 (Southeast Asia 2)

Consignees who are subscribed to APL's a_____④_____(到货通知) will be notified of any d_____⑤_____(迟延) in vessel ETA exceeding 24 hours against their respective shipment. In addition, real-time container level details can be found on APL's HomePort web portal *www.apl.com*.

If you have any queries, kindly c_____⑥_____(联系) your local APL customer service representative.

Sincerely,

APL Co., Ltd

Unit 12　Cargo Damage and Claim
　　（货损及索赔）

Cargo Damage and Claim
（货损及索赔） Unit 12

Part A: Basic Knowledge Concerned

Text 1: The Causes of Cargo Damage

The container revolution of the 1960s was deemed to be the solution to limiting cargo damage, but has experience proved otherwise?

A considerable proportion of the UK Club's time is taken up handling container cargo claims where 25% of the damage is physical, 14% temperature related, 11% containers lost overboard, 9% theft and 8% shortage.

The graph below shows how these compare to damages of all the UK Club's large cargo claims and highlights some of the real benefits, or otherwise, of containerization.

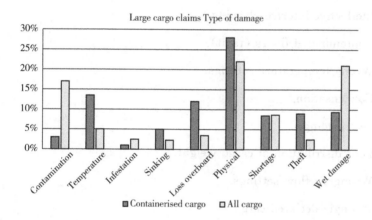

It is worrying that one of the biggest contributory causes of container cargo damage is bad stowage—causing nearly 20% of the claims. It would seem that we have merely shifted the cargo damage problem further back up the transit chain.

Shore error now accounts for around 27% of large container cargo claims compared with 19% for all types of cargo claim, tie this in with bad stowage statistics and it seems to point to problems originating at the time of stuffing.

We seem to have substituted problems in one large container (the ship) to problems in a lot of smaller containers (the container). With around 12,000,000 containers in circulation and 95,000,000 loaded container movements each year, this seems to be a real problem for the industry.

Although it is a major cause of container cargo damage, it would be wrong to lay the origin of all container cargo claims on bad stowage alone. Listed below are many other reasons for damage:

- Lack of export packaging.
- Increased use of weak retail packaging.
- Inadequate ventilation.
- Wrong choice of container.
- Poor condition of container.
- Lack of effective container interchange inspection.
- Ineffective sealing arrangements.
- Lack of clear carriage instructions.
- Ineffective internal cleaning.
- Contaminated floors (taint).
- Wrong temperature settings.
- Condensation.
- Overloading.
- Poor distribution of cargo weight.
- Wrong air flow settings.
- Wrongly declared cargo.
- B/L temperature notations misleading/unachievable.
- Lack of reefer points.
- Organized crime.
- Heavy containers stowed on light.
- Stack weights exceeded.
- Heat sensitive cargoes stowed on/adjacent to heated bunker tanks or in direct sunlight.
- Fragile* cargoes stowed in areas of high motion.
- Damaged, worn, mixed securing equipment.
- Poor monitoring of temperatures.

fragile
adj. 脆的，易碎的

- Wrong use of temperature controls.

As an insurer finding and highlighting the problems and where the money goes is easy. Rectifying those problems unfortunately is not.

Text 2: Marine Cargo Claims Guide

Background and Purpose

MCC Transport continuously strives to improve our customer service. Any situation that gives rise to a cargo claim is by nature* trying. We will do our utmost to minimize your inconvenience. We have prepared this guide to avoid misunderstandings about our claims handling process and to make the process as efficient and simple as possible.

> by nature
> 天生，生性

Steps You Should Take

1. Notify your insurance underwriter*.

> underwriter
> n. 保险人（公司）

If damage or loss to your cargo is apparent upon receipt, you should notify your cargo insurance underwriters immediately. They will advise you how to comply with all procedures required to fully protect your insurance coverage.

2. Contact MCC Customer Service.

At the same time, you should also contact your local MCC Transport Customer Service so that we may assist you in the most effective manner. You should do so immediately (within 3 days after delivery) because a late notification will adversely* affect your legal position. Late notification may also make it difficult to identify the exact condition of the cargo on delivery and to distinguish between the damage that may have occurred while in MCC's care and any possible aggravated* damage after delivery.

> adversely
> adj. 不利地

> aggravate
> v. 加重，使恶化

When contacting us, we would ask that you please have the following information readily available:

When you give us...	It helps us to...
• MCC Transport Document number • Container number • Cargo description	Identify the specific shipment at issue
Nature of the cargo damage/loss	Determine the course of investigation
Approximate value of damage/loss	Communicate properly with our own insurers

3. Engage a surveyor if necessary.

Please note that you are not required to engage a surveyor if you already have other document can show the extent of the loss and the root cause. There are, however, benefits in engaging one. Independent marine surveyors are professionals who are well-versed* in examining damaged cargo and surrounding circumstances. They may spot* issues, facts or conditions which an untrained eye may miss. In addition, they can often assist in loss mitigation*.

The surveyors will summarize their findings in a report, which may form the basis for your claim for compensation from MCC. You should weigh the expense of surveyors against the benefit of their work, product and expertise, and make your decisions accordingly.

Preferably, the survey should be undertaken jointly with a separate surveyor appointed by MCC. If possible, the survey should take place while the cargo is still untouched in the container so as to provide the surveyors the opportunity to observe the cargo's stowage, bracing and blocking*, damage pattern, and other points of interest.

4. Mitigate* cargo loss.

Please note that as a matter of law, you MUST do your utmost to mitigate your loss. Such measures may include precautions to protect the value of sound cargo by segregating* the damaged cargo. Damaged cargo may be salvaged for sale in secondary markets. There may be alternate use for damaged goods. Repair or cure may also be possible, which may prove more economical and timely than re-ordering the same goods. Please keep the salvage* invoice (issued by independent third party) to us as evidence of loss mitigation.

Reasonable costs incurred in mitigation of loss may be included in your claim.

5. Collect documents.

You should take pictures of the sound cargo as well as the damaged cargo (so that we may compare them). The pictures should show not only the packaging or exterior of the damaged cargo but also the damaged goods or products. You should also take pictures of the container(s)—particularly if there is container damage — including a picture showing the container number(s). You should keep these

---

well-versed
adj. 精通的，熟知的

spot
v. 认出，识别出

mitigation
n. 减轻

bracing and blocking
支撑和阻塞

mitigate
v. 减轻

segregating
v. 使隔离，使分离

salvage
n. 救助，打捞

pictures as evidence in the event that it becomes necessary for you to file a formal claim.

For reefer shipments, record the temperature, humidity and ventilation settings (if applicable) as well.

6. Submit a quantified* claim.

quantified
adj. 量化的，定量的

Your formal claim should be submitted on your company letterhead, and include an itemized* claim statement and calculation with the specific value of cargo damage or loss. It should also include the documents or items described in the table below. We refer to complete and well-supported claims as quantified claims.

itemized
adj. 详细列明的

We request	Because it helps us to...
MCC Transport Document number	Identify the specific shipment at issue
Commercial invoice of the shipment	Substantiate the value of the cargo
Packing list of the shipment	Validate the cargo count and content
Survey report with original & colour photographs	Assess the extent of damage or loss
Calculation of claim	Match against submitted documentation
Salvage invoice or destruction certificate	Confirm reasonable mitigation efforts or destruction

Depending on the nature of your claim, we may request additional information, such as:	Because it helps us to...
Stuffing report	Assess the cargo's stowage
Temperature records (if applicable)	Assess any deviation in cargo temperature
Unloading tally	Substantiate cargo quantity at de-stuffing
Delivery receipt	Verify receipt, check seal integrity and examine any exceptions
Equipment interchange receipts	Verify container handover, check seal integrity and examine any exceptious
Export/import declaration	Corroborate cargo, quantity and/or value

Notes: These documents may be known by different names.

7. Protect against time bar*.

time bar
时效

In most cases, your claim is subject to a one-year statute of limitations, or time bar. If your claim should remain unresolved after one year from the date of delivery (or intended delivery if the shipment was lost), you must request, in writing, time extension to MCC and get confirmation from MCC by return. If you fail to take this step, our obligation to handle your claim will expire.

MCC Transport strictly enforces this right as required by our insurance arrangement and auditing standards.

Steps We Will Take

1. Acknowledge receipt of your claim notification.

2. Engage a surveyor if necessary.

3. Initiate an investigation of the cause of damage.

4. Await your quantified claim.

5. Acknowledge receipt of your quantified claim and request any missing documentation.

6. Finalize our internal investigation.

7. Evaluate the Merits of your claim and the extent of MCC Transport's liability.

8. Communicate the result of our investigation to you.

Please bear in mind that the critical event in the handling of your claim is receipt of your quantified claim—this will help us identify any other relevant facts and conduct additional investigations as needed. Once our investigation is finalized, we will evaluate the merits of your claim in the light of all relevant facts and in accordance with the terms and conditions of our contract of carriage and applicable law and/or international carriage of goods conventions.

invoke
v. 引起

We appreciate that some of the defences that may be invoked* in our evaluation of your claim may not be common knowledge and may even sound foreign. However, cargo underwriters are well-versed in these provisions and will be able to deal with them efficiently and effectively. Please bear this in mind when deciding whether you should insure your cargo or not.

Part B: Business Letters

Sample 1: Notice of Intent to Claim

To: XYZ Shipping Line

Attn: Claims Department

Cargo Damage and Claim
（货损及索赔） Unit 12

RE:

Vessel name: AAA

Voyage number: 011E

Place of Origin to Place of Destination:

Shipper: ABC Company

Bill of Lading No. and Date: XYZ1666888, 10 September 2017

Description of Claim and Cargo: 50 cartons package broken, total 1000 pieces of footwear in loss

The captioned shipment has been received short and/or damaged for which we hold you fully responsible. As soon as the extent of the loss is determined, a detailed claim will be submitted.

Please acknowledge receipt of this letter by return facsimile/letter.

Yours faithfully,

XXX (company name)

Sample 2: Extension of Suit time (For Ocean Shipment Only)

To: XYZ Shipping Line

Attn: Claims Department

RE:

Vessel name: AAA

Voyage number: 011E

Place of Origin to Place of Destination: Yantian, GD, PRC to Los Angeles, CA, USA

Shipper: ABC Company

Bill of Lading No. and Date: XYZ1666888, 10 September 2017

Description of Claim and Cargo: 50 cartons package broken, total 1000 pieces of footwear in loss

We request that you, on behalf of the owners and/or charters of the vessel AAA provide us with extension in which commence suit up to and including November 11, 2017.

Kindly acknowledge agreement and sign the enclosed copy, and return to our offices as soon as possible.

Yours faithfully,

XXX (company name)

Sample 3: Freight Claim Declination Letter

Dear Sir,

We have received your letter of 15th June, informing us that the crockery we shipped to you arrived in damaged condition on account of improper stowage.

Upon receipt of your letter, we gave this matter our immediate attention. We have studied your surveyor's report* very carefully.

We are convinced that the present damage was due to extraordinary circumstances under which they were transported to you. We are therefore not responsible for the damage; but as we do not think that it would be fair to have you bear the loss alone, we suggest that the loss be divided between both of us, to which we hope you will agree.

Yours faithfully,

XXX (company name)

surveyor's report
检验报告

Part C: Situational Dialogue

扫码听音频

Scene 1: Talking About Cause of Damage

Mr. Taylor is invited to Mr. Wu's office to discuss what to do with the damaged machine his company delivered.

Wu: I must say, Mr. Taylor, your deliveries have so far been satisfactory. But, the SW-3 machine was found damaged on delivery yesterday.

Taylor: I'm sorry to hear that. Have your people at the port determined the cause of the damage?

Cargo Damage and Claim （货损及索赔） Unit 12

Wu: Yes, they have. Damage to the machine is due to violent bumping before loading.

Taylor: On what ground did they come to the conclusion?

Wu: Because the containing case is broken and patched*.

patch
v. 修补

Taylor: Breakage never happened to our deliveries before. And, our machine exports have so far been packed in the same way using the same quality cases. The damage might have been caused by rough handling*.

rough handling
野蛮操作

Wu: Do you mean before or after loading?

Taylor: As the Bill of Lading is not claused to that effect, the accident should have happened after loading on the sea voyage. In that case, the insurance company should be held responsible.

Wu: The inspection report here denies that possibility. (*Reading*) "As a result of careful checking and testing, it is found that the plywood board patched on one side of Case 20/42 and the nails driven on the board are not made in China. This proves that the case had been broken and patched before loading".

Taylor: That can only prove the containing case had been patched before loading. Damage to the machine could have occurred on the rough sea.

Wu: That possibility is also excluded. (*Reading*) "The above vessel did not encounter bad weather during its voyage according to the Log Book*."

Log Book
航海日志

Taylor: Then, is it possible that the machine was bumped and damaged on delivery?

Wu: The inspection report says that the Tally Sheet* at destination had been checked and no remarks about damage by rough handling were recorded.

Tally Sheet
理货单

Taylor: Well, let's hear the conclusion of the report.

Wu: It says "Case 20/42 containing the SW-3 Machine had been damaged and patched before loading. Damage to the machine is due to violent bumping before shipment."

Taylor: I think I have no more questions. Now, Mr. Wu, How would you like the matter to be settled?

Wu: We'd like to replace the damaged machine.

Taylor: As our engineer for the trial run will fly in tomorrow, can't we wait until he's here? We'll surely settle the matter to your satisfaction.

Wu: All right, Mr. Taylor. Let's meet again tomorrow.

Scene 2: A Clerk Discusses an Insurance Claim with His Boss

A: What is your hurry?

B: Bad news! That shipment of parts from Japan has been partially lost and damaged at sea. What should we do when loss or damage occurs?

A: We must prepare our claim and send it to the underwriter to secure payment.

B: Won't our broker take care of that?

A: Yes, that is part of the service on the broker's side.

B: So the first step would be to contact our broker?

A: Yes, and we'll need to submit some documents to him.

B: Is it enough that we have an on-board Bill of Lading to claim settlement?

A: I'm sorry to say it isn't. We'll need a statement from the shipping agents stating that the goods were actually loaded and noting when the vessel sailed. We'll also need to present proof of ownership.

B: How do we do that?

A: We'll have to file a full original set of ocean Bills of Lading, the insurance certificate, and the original commercial invoice.

B: No Problem. I have them on file.

A: We may also need a statement of protest.

B: What is that?

A: It is usually an exact from the ship's logbook which describes how the goods were lost or damaged. It's prepared by the master of the vessel. Sometimes that documentation is also required.

B: Well, that covers all the things I want to know. I guess I'll call our broker.

A: Yes, let's get started right away.

Part D: Related Documents

Sample: Statement of Claim

Standard Form for Presentation of Loss and Damage Claims

(Company name of Claimant) (Address of claimant)	(Claimant's Number)*
(Name of Carrier) (Date)	(PRO Number)
(Address)	

This claim for $_____ is made against the carrier named above by _____
(Amount of claim) (Name of Claimant)
for _____ in connection with the following described shipment(s):
(Loss or damage)
Description of shipment _____
Name and address of consignor (shipper) _____
Shipped from _____, to _____
(City, Town or Station) (City, Town, or Station)
Final Destination _____ Routed via _____
(City, Town or Station)
Bill of lading issued by: _____ Date of Bill of Lading: _____
Paid Freight Bill (Pro) Number: _____
Name and address of Consignee (Whom shipped to) _____
If shipment reconsigned enroute, state particulars: _____

DETAILED STATEMENT SHOWING HOW AMOUNT CLAIMED IS DETERMINED
(Number and Description of articles, nature and extent of loss or damage, invoice price of articles, amount of claim, etc.)

Total Amount Claimed

IN ADDITION TO THE INFORMATION GIVEN ABOVE, THE FOLLOWING DOCUMENTS ARE SUBMITTED IN SUPPORT OF THIS CLAIM**

( ) 1. Original bill of lading, if not previously surrendered to carrier.
( ) 2. Original paid freight ("expense") bill.
( ) 3. Original invoice or certified copy showing claimants cost.
( ) 4. Other particulars obtainable in proof of loss or damage claimed.

Remarks: _____

The foregoing statements of facts is hereby certified to as correct.

_____   _____
Printed name of claimant (print clearly)
(Claimants contact phone number)   (Signature of claimant)

*Claimant should assign to each claim a number, inserting same in the space provided at the upper right hand corner of this form. Reference should be made thereto in all correspondence pertaining to this claim.
**Claimant will please place check (X) before such of the documents mentioned as have been attached, and explain under "Remarks" the absence of any of the documents called for in connection with this claim. When for any reason it is impossible for claimant to produce original bill of lading, or paid freight bill, claimant should indemnify carrier or carriers against duplicate claim supported by original documents.

Exercises

Task 1: Listen to the following text and fill in each blank with one or two appropriate words.

Though all necessary precautionary steps to prevent cargo damage may have been taken, it is not always possible to eliminate damage altogether in maritime transport. Cargo damage commonly occurs in loading, discharging or carriage, and it takes many ___①___, such as original damage, stevedore damage, heavy weather damage, sweat damage, ___②___ damage, and damage arising from inherent nature or vice of goods. It is important to note that the carrier has the burden of proving the cause of the loss or damage is one of the excepted ___③___. This will mean that the carrier must prove how the damage occurred. Additionally, where the damage is caused by two or more causes, one of which is excluded and the other is not, the carrier must ___④___ between the damages caused by the excepted peril and the damages caused by the non-excepted peril. If the carrier cannot make this distinction, he is probably liable for the whole damage. It is further important to remember that the carrier cannot rely upon any of the excepted perils if a cause of the damage failed to exercise due diligence to make the vessel ___⑤___.

Neither the carrier nor the ship shall be responsible for loss or damage or delay arising or resulting from the following circumstances: Act of God; Perils, dangers, and accidents of the sea or other navigable water; war, hostilities, armed conflict, ___⑥___, terrorism, riots, and civil commotions; ___⑦___ restrictions; interference by or impediments created by governments, public authorities, rulers, or people including detention, arrest, or seizure not attributable to the carrier; ___⑧___, lockouts, stoppage, or restraints of labor; fire on the ship; ___⑨___ defects not discoverable by due diligence; act or ___⑩___ of the shipper, the documentary shipper, the controlling party, or any other person for whose acts the shipper or the documentary shipper is liable; loading, handling, stowing, or unloading of the goods performed pursuant to the relative agreement, unless the carrier or performing party performs such activity on behalf of the shipper, the documentary shipper, or the consignee; wastage in bulk or weight or any other loss or damage arising from inherent ___⑪___, quality, or vice of the goods; insufficiency or defective condition of ___⑫___ or marking not performed by or on behalf of the carrier; saving or attempting to save ___⑬___ at sea; reasonable measures to save or attempt to save ___⑭___ at sea; and reasonable measures to avoid or attempt to avoid damage to the ___⑮___.

Cargo Damage and Claim
（货损及索赔） Unit 12

Task 2: Fill in each blank with the most appropriate word given below in its right form.

untouched	survey	course	cause	submit
settle	lodge	intentional	sound	validity

1. The investigation shows that the damage to the insured goods was _____ by natural calamities; therefore your company is liable for the loss.

2. The shortage of the insured goods arose from external causes in the _____ of transit; therefore you shall be responsible for the total loss.

3. According to our on-the-spot investigation the damage was caused by the _____ act of the insured, so the company is free from any responsibility for it.

4. You should take pictures of the _____ cargo as well as the damaged cargo (so that we may compare them).

5. You should have applied for _____ as soon as the insured goods were found to have sustained loss. We are sorry that you failed to do so.

6. If possible, the survey should take place while the cargo is still _____ in the container so as to provide the surveyors the opportunity to observe the cargo's stowage, bracing and blocking, damage pattern, and other points of interest.

7. You should _____ a claim with the carrier or the party concerned in writing.

8. You have exceeded the time of _____ of a claim.

9. What documents shall I _____ when I present a claim to your company?

10. We sincerely hope our disputes would be _____ by friendly negotiation on principles of seeking truth from facts and of fairness and reasonableness.

Task 3: Translate the following terms.

1. Actual total loss
2. Insurance underwriter
3. Mitigate cargo loss
4. Marine surveyor
5. File a formal claim

6. 合理费用
7. 检验报告
8. 时效
9. 索赔通知
10. 货损原因

Task 4: Complete the following letters according to the Chinese words and expressions given in brackets.

Dear Sir,

We thank you for your letter of August 10, together with supporting documents c____①____

(索赔) compensation for shortage of five cartons from the above c_____②_____ (托运物).

We have looked into this matter and would state that the goods were stowed, dunnaged and separated according to the requirements and customs of the trade and that special watchmen, officers, crew members and sometimes even armed policemen were employed to watch the cargo during the vessel's s_____③_____ (停留) in way ports in order to prevent p_____④_____ (偷盗).

Therefore, the vessel has exercised due care and done everything that can reasonably be expected to protect your cargo. When, in spite of all these p_____⑤_____ (预防措施), five cartons are found to have been pilfered, we hold that this can't be regarded as a l_____⑥_____ (缺乏) of due diligence.

In this particular case, however, we shall be prepared to s_____⑦_____ (理赔) your claim by paying 50% of the amount claimed in full.

We return your debit note for alternation.

Yours faithfully,

XXX (company name)

Keys to the Exercises

Unit 1 Overview of Container Shipping

Task 1: Listening

①advantages ②adoption ③rate ④damage
⑤eliminated ⑥transit ⑦efficient ⑧freight cost
⑨machinery ⑩transferred ⑪stacked ⑫applications

Task 2: Vocabulary

1. regular 2. capacity 3. integration 4. equivalent
5. competitive 6. share 7. overcapacity 8. weekly
9. charter 10. variety

Task 3: Terms Translation

1. 航运联盟
2. 集装箱化
3. 船舶经营人
4. 二氧化碳排放
5. 船舶共享协议
6. mode of transport
7. liner service/liner transportation
8. ocean carrier
9. supply chain
10. container ship

Task 4: Complete Business Letters

①effect ②alliance ③unaffected ④deployed
⑤reliable ⑥liner ⑦commitments ⑧support

Unit 2 Cargo Canvassing

Task 1: Listening

①tariff ②ports ③competition ④range
⑤volume ⑥destination ⑦gross weight ⑧date of shipment
⑨Collect

Task 2: Vocabulary

1. shipper 2. freight rate 3. canvassing 4. service contract

5. Tariff   6. TEU   7. General Rate Increase

8. effect   9. applicable   10. quoted

Task 3：Terms Translation

1. 运价表费率   8. contract rate

2. 海运费报价   9. Bunker Adjustment Factor

3. 普遍运价上涨   10. Terminal Handling Charge

4. 业务拜访   11. Peak Season Surcharge

5. 未付的运费   12. Shipping market

6. 客户档案   13. Service Contract

7. 航运周刊   14. Sailing schedule/Vessel schedule

Task 4：Complete Business Letters

①situation   ②incurred   ③trigger   ④effective

⑤applicable   ⑥resolve   ⑦normal   ⑧quantum

⑨understanding   ⑩surcharge

Unit 3　Booking Acceptance

Task 1：Listening

①Frequency   ②quotation   ③subject   ④separate

⑤specific   ⑥Source   ⑦Prompt   ⑧lasting

⑨goodwill

Task 2：Vocabulary

1. Subject   2. ETA   3. Shipping order   4. shipping space

5. carrier   6. sailing schedule   7. port rotation   8. transit times

9. frequencies   10. unbalanced

Task 3：Terms Translation

1. 订舱单   6. Transit Time

2. 订舱确认单   7. Booking Party

Keys to the Exercises

3. 船期表

4. 港口顺序

5. 预计离港时间/预计到港时间

8. Shipping space

9. Shipping order

10. Place of receipt

Task 4: Complete Business Letters

①advised ②replaced ③booked ④transferred

⑤hesitate

Unit 4 Empty Container Release

Task 1: Listening

①divided ②shipping line ③accept ④move

⑤improper packing ⑥applicable ⑦railed ⑧road

⑨nominated ⑩negotiate ⑪liability ⑫delivery

Task 2: Vocabulary

1. pick-up 2. depots 3. enhance 4. standards

5. accommodating 6. inspector 7. payload 8. reveal

9. defects 10. exercise

Task 3: Terms Translation

1. 集装箱堆场

2. 提箱

3. 还箱

4. 内陆运输

5. 货主拖车

6. carrier's haulage

7. EIR (Equipment Interchange Receipt)

8. Empty Container

9. Full container/laden container

10. container inspection

Task 4: Complete Business Letters

①objective ②release ③appointed ④cooperation

⑤sound ⑥picking up ⑦reject ⑧take photos

⑨assistance

Unit 5 Containers Stuffing

Task 1: Listening

①transshipment   ②play   ③take charge of   ④consigne

⑤intact   ⑥Carrier   ⑦good condition   ⑧terms

⑨variety   ⑩delivery methods   ⑪preferable

Task 2: Vocabulary

1. secured   2. load   3. crushing   4. dry

5. dunnage   6. evenly   7. compliance   8. improper

9. bottom   10. liquid

Task 3: Terms Translation

1. 装箱计划   6. pallet

2. 装箱单   7. wooden packing

3. 载重量   8. container capacity

4. 包装不固   9. dunnage

5. 集装箱底板   10. carton

Task 4: Complete Business Letter

①advise   ②left   ③space   ④capacity

⑤hold

Unit 6 Laden Containers Gate-in

Task 1: Listening

①safety   ②slow down   ③fastened   ④entry

⑤exit   ⑥empty chassis   ⑦approval   ⑧reversing

⑨designated   ⑩passageways   ⑪cranes   ⑫operators

⑬traffic signs

Task 2: Vocabulary

1. weigh   2. shut-out   3. Overweight   4. stacked

5. chassis   6. verifying   7. scaled   8. vessel planner

9. reloaded   10. dock receipt

Task 3: Terms Translation

1. 核定的集装箱总重
2. 滞期费
3. 滞柜费
4. 开舱日
5. 集装箱返还堆场
6. Dock Receipt
7. Berth Allocation
8. Equipment Interchange Receipt
9. entry gate lane
10. Container Yard

Task 4: Complete Business Letter

①adopted   ②verify   ③packed   ④condition
⑤breach   ⑥mass   ⑦weighed   ⑧added
⑨standards   ⑩declaration   ⑪guidelines

Unit 7 Customs Clearance

Task 1: Listening

①step   ②testifies   ③accordance   ④import
⑤in transit   ⑥certificates   ⑦applicant   ⑧weight
⑨health   ⑩origin   ⑪value   ⑫compulsory
⑬absence   ⑭sample   ⑮lower   ⑯manufacturing
⑰designated

Task 2: Vocabulary

1. present   2. classified   3. waiver   4. cut-off
5. infectious   6. exemption   7. identical   8. data
9. revoked   10. lodged

Task 3: Terms Translation

1. 出口许可
2. 商品检验
3. 报检员
4. 进出境
6. customs declaration
7. customs specialist
8. packing list
9. commercial invoice

5. 报检委托书

10. bonded goods

Task 4: Complete Business Letters

①issued　　　②advance　　　③fill　　　④submitting

⑤result in　　⑥implementation

Unit 8　Cargo Handling at Container Port

Task 1: Listening

①entrusted　　　②carefully　　　③holds　　　④residue

⑤made out　　　⑥broken stowage　⑦reverse　　⑧stability

⑨blocked off　　⑩compatible　　⑪load-line　⑫application

Task 2: Vocabulary

1. TEU　　　2. order　　　3. reverse　　　4. stowage

5. accessible　6. transfer　　7. draft　　　8. loaded

9. handling　　10. congestion

Task 3: Terms Translation

1. 积载图　　　　　　　　6. stevedore

2. 贝位图　　　　　　　　7. straddle carrier

3. 贝/列/层　　　　　　　8. reach stacker

4. 集装箱堆场　　　　　　9. loading and unloading

5. 捆绑和系固　　　　　　10. marshalling yard

Task 4: Complete Business Letters

①pleasure　　　②rendered　　　③assure　　　④appointed

⑤useful　　　　⑥inquire

Unit 9　Tally Work

Task 1: Listening

①in case　　　②original　　　③compiling　　　④terminal operator

⑤receipt ⑥check ⑦reseal ⑧blame for
⑨inspection ⑩on deck ⑪make up ⑫immediate
⑬commenced ⑭transshipment ⑮confirming ⑯rests on

Task 2: Vocabulary

1. legal 2. supply 3. counting 4. progress
5. distinguish 6. stand 7. divided 8. course
9. loading 10. inspecting

Task 3: Terms Translation

1. 理货单
2. 装船清单
3. 岸吊
4. 进口舱单
5. 货损类别
6. restow container
7. tallyman
8. chief mate/chief officer
9. transshipment container
10. gang

Task 4: Complete Business Letters

①requirements ②broken ③crew ④free
⑤shortage

Unit 10　B/L Issuance

Task 1: Listening

①maritime ②shipper ③order ④loading
⑤freight ⑥mode ⑦particulars ⑧purposes
⑨evidence ⑩title ⑪accomplished ⑫first
⑬ensure ⑭non-negotiable

Task 2: Vocabulary

1. clean 2. title 3. order 4. exchange
5. negotiable 6. surrendered 7. indemnified 8. gross
9. canceled 10. cut-off

Task 3: Terms Translation

1. 货代提单/分提单
2. 托运人
3. 收货人
4. 通知人
5. 运费到付

6. sea waybill
7. anti-dated B/L
8. straight B/L
9. freight prepaid
10. order B/L

Task 4: Complete Business Letters

①inform   ②control   ③delivery   ④liable
⑤operators   ⑥agents   ⑦risk   ⑧ceases
⑨obtain   ⑩accept

Unit 11 Cargo Arrival and Delivery

Task 1: Listening

①location   ②stacked   ③crane   ④cargo plan
⑤weight   ⑥evenly   ⑦unbalanced   ⑧stevedores
⑨hook up   ⑩spreader   ⑪locked   ⑫straddle carrier
⑬storage area   ⑭middle   ⑮crew   ⑯ballast tanks

Task 2: Vocabulary

1. release
2. go through
3. rely on
4. transfer
5. congestion
6. schedule
7. berth
8. acknowledged
9. attention
10. failure

Task 3: Terms Translation

1. 小陆桥
2. 提货单
3. 到货通知
4. 电放
5. 交货凭证

6. import license
7. import cargo manifest
8. import clearance
9. letter of indemnity, letter of guarantee
10. devanning/unstuffing of containers

Task 4: Complete Business Letters

①congestion　　②berth　　③shortage　　④arrival notice
⑤delay　　⑥contact

Unit 12　Cargo Damage and Claim

Task 1: Listening

①forms　　②pilferage　　③perils　　④distinguish
⑤seaworthy　　⑥piracy　　⑦quarantine　　⑧strikes
⑨latent　　⑩omission　　⑪defect　　⑫packing
⑬life　　⑭property　　⑮environment

Task 2: Vocabulary

1. caused   2. course   3. intentional   4. sound
5. survey   6. untouched   7. lodge   8. validity
9. submit   10. settled

Task 3: Terms Translation

1. 实际全损
2. 保险人/保险公司
3. 减少货物的损失
4. 海事检验师
5. 提出正式索赔
6. reasonable cost
7. survey report
8. time bar
9. claim notification
10. cause of cargo damage

Task 4: Complete Business Letters

①claiming　　②consignment　　③stay　　④pilferage
⑤precautions　　⑥lack　　⑦settle

References

[1] 袁洪林. 国际船舶代理业务实用英语会话[M]. 大连：大连海事大学出版社，2007.

[2] 赵鲁克. 外轮理货英语[M]. 上海：复旦大学出版社，2011.

[3] 赵鲁克. 港口理货英语[M]. 北京：人民交通出版社股份有限公司，2015.

[4] 杨丹凤. 远洋运输业务英语[M]. 上海：复旦大学出版社，2015.

[5] 司玉琢. 海事实用英语大全[M]. 2版. 大连：大连海事大学出版社，2000.

[6] 陈丹，李硕. 秀出一口好英语丛书：物流英语脱口秀[M]. 北京：北京师范大学出版社，2013.

[7] 荣瑾. 报关与国际货运专业英语[M]. 北京：中国海关出版社，2014.

[8] 陈鑫，李富森. 报关与国际货运专业英语[M]. 天津：天津大学出版社，2010.

[9] 范苗福. 国际航运业务英语与函电[M]. 大连：大连海事大学出版社，2000.

[10] 中国外轮代理总公司. 国际航运代理业务英语函电[M]. 大连：大连海运学院出版社，1992.

[11] 王晓萍. 国际港航英语[M]. 杭州：浙江大学出版社，2013.